Advance

"*The Zone of Connection* is beautifully constructed and
a powerful advocacy for connection. It is most timely in
a world that seems to generate increasing fragmentation
within and between us. Drawing on their own personal
journeys and enquiries, Sue and Penny offer us with heartfelt
care and compassion both a coherent synthesis of knowledge
and wisdom, ancient and modern, and a practical pathway
forward. To relate we must connect, to heal we must
connect, to be fulfilled we must connect. I encourage
you to connect with this book."

Paul King, executive and embodiment coach and trainer,
and founder of The Beyond Partnership

"I would trust these two wonderful women with the fate of
the world in their hands. They demonstrate in their lives such
authenticity, integrity, passion, power and connection that they
can't help but touch and transform your life for the better. You
couldn't be in better hands traversing the Zone of Connection."

Soleira Green, transformationalist
and author of *The Genius Game*

"Sue and Penny's book provides a deeply authentic and comprehensive approach to creating the future you want to experience, a future that brings a deep sense of wellbeing to your life. Go online and get it now. It will change your life."

Richard Barrett, founder of the Barrett Values Centre and author of *A New Psychology of Human Well-Being*

"I wish I had had these tools while I was a principal ballerina. So much about performing on stage is affected by our state of mind. This book will take you to a zone of peak performance, where you will connect with who you really are – beyond stress, struggle and the need for approval – to reach your audience with your head, heart and whole being. My new ritual of exercise is the Connection Practice. It has brought me balance and confidence and had an amazing effect on my whole life."

Leanne Benjamin AM OBE, former principal dancer with the Royal Ballet, Covent Garden

"This book is a great guide for people on a personal development journey who want to accelerate their growth. The exercises will enable you to improve your presence and radiate positive energy. I recommend it to anyone who has already tried mindfulness and wants to move beyond that."

Stephanie Hale, author of *Millionaire Author* and *How to Sell One Million Books*

"*The Zone of Connection* is a practical guide that shows you how to connect with the universal energy flow that will literally turbocharge your life and transform how you feel. The majority of people remain unaware of the innate power they have access to. Crammed with fascinating theories, tips and exercises, it blends neuroscience with a range of esoteric teachings presented in an easy-to-read way. I absolutely loved it."

Nikki Owen, thought leader on authentic charism, award-winning speaker and author of *Charismatic to the Core*

"Sue and Penny offer a refreshingly grounded approach to energy work and personal development, taking complex ideas and making them user-friendly. This practical book supports your journey inward, connecting you with your inner wisdom and enhancing your overall wellbeing. Highly recommended."

Caroline Shola Arewa, award-winning wellness coach trainer and author of *Energy 4 Life*

"Inspiring, funny and fascinating – this book will help you to reconnect to who you really are and discover how you can become the truly amazing person that you are destined to be. Powerful stuff, well-researched and very easy to read. This book will help you to experience a new and more powerful way of living. Five stars."

Sophie Bennett, bestselling author of *Find Your Flame: Why Motivation Matters More Than Talent* and keynote speaker

"Transforming and life changing! A visionary approach to finding happiness within. A brilliant book for these disconnected times."

Dennie Gordon, film and television director, *Ally McBeal*, *White Collar* and *What a Girl Wants*

"In a world where many people are evermore subconsciously disconnected, this book offers a practical, no-nonsense guide as to how one can reconnect with the self and learn how to live in the moment. Refreshingly, *The Zone of Connection* is not only research based, but importantly experience based. A book to go back to again and again."

Tony Kosoko, specialist musculoskeletal physiotherapist, The Practice

"The human species exists with an extraordinary absurdity. We are living lives that are very disconnected and yet scientists and mystics tell us that the ultimate reality and truth is that we are all deeply connected, not just with ourselves and others but with all life, animate and inanimate. This book is a significant contribution in helping us to be more connected, i.e., to return to our true state. It is comprehensive, accessible, fun, inspiring and very informative. I thoroughly recommend it."

Andrew Wallas, individual and corporate shaman, Business Alchemy

"You're looking for clarity? Look no farther than this beautiful book overflowing with insight, honesty, wisdom and humanity. Uplifting, inspiring, enlightening – but best of all – practical and effective. Where has this book been all my life?"

Rikki Beadle-Blaire MBE, artistic director, Team Angelica

"This book unpacks the secret of living from your full intelligence, true power and deep capacity for relationship. You can be free of limited, past-based patterns to effortlessly and joyfully create the life you want."

Jenny Garrett, executive coach, leadership trainer and author of *Rocking Your Role*

"Keeping your operating system up to date in today's rapidly changing world is difficult. So, if you want to stay ahead of the game and be the best version of yourself, this book, *The Zone of Connection*, is definitely for you."

Lady Shaw Ruddock CBE, London-based philanthropist, former investment banker and author of *The Second Half of Your Life*

"I've had the pleasure of participating in a truly electrifying workshop with this dynamic, inspiring and compassionate duo, and I'm overjoyed they've now given birth to this wonderful book. We live in challenging and unusual times, mental health issues are rife, we feel increasingly disconnected from nature, and society is marked by separation, fragmentation and polarization. Yet beneath it all, we are indeed interconnected. If you want a map and tools with which to successfully navigate these times with love, deepening your connections, taking basic mindfulness skills to a whole new level so you can experience the fully conscious life that is your birthright, you've come to the right place."

Liz Hall, author of *Mindful Coaching*, mindfulness teacher, trainer and coach, and editor of *Coaching at Work* magazine

"A really easy-to-use guide to finding your energy flow state written from two lifetimes of wisdom and experience. Sue and Penny have been inspiring and helping others to live, create and achieve their goals for many years and this book is a product of their vast knowledge. Many of us feel separate from everything, and Sue and Penny have given us a wonderful tool to keep us conscious that we are all connected and in that zone we are limitless."

Ted Wilmont, master practitioner and trainer, EFTMRA

Published by
LID Publishing Limited
The Record Hall, Studio 204,
16-16a Baldwins Gardens,
London EC1N 7RJ, UK

524 Broadway, 11th Floor, Suite 08-120,
New York, NY 10012, US

info@lidpublishing.com
www.lidpublishing.com

A member of:

Business Publishers Roundtable
www.businesspublishersroundtable.com

Printed in Latvia by Jelgavas Tipogrāfij
ISBN: 978-1-912555-19-2

Cover and page design: Matthew Renaudin

SHIFT YOUR ENERGY TO **HAPPINESS,
LOVE AND BEYOND**

THE ZONE OF
CONNECTION

**PENNY MALLINSON
& SUE COYNE**

LONDON   NEW YORK   SHANGHAI
MADRID   BARCELONA   BOGOTA
MEXICO CITY   MONTERREY   BUENOS AIRES

We dedicate this book to all those who have the courage to make the journey to find out who they really are.

Contents

List of Exercises

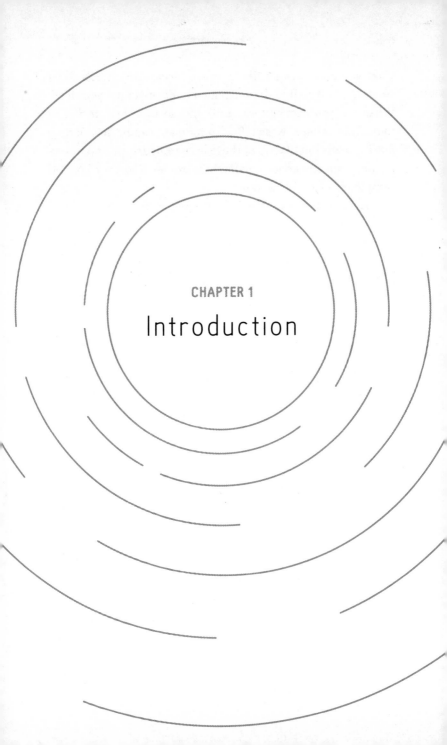

CHAPTER 1

Introduction

Have you ever felt that life is near perfect, everything's going your way, only to find the rug pulled out from under your feet? Whatever you thought was safe and secure, your rock and foundation, simply wasn't. Such a moment can be devastating, but it can also mark one of those extraordinary, pivotal events in life when someone or something comes into your life and completely changes its course.

That happened to us. Back in 2004, when we – Sue and Penny – met, we were two women who had a lot in common. We both had children of the same age and successful business careers, and we had each been part of a power couple with our husbands. We had created beautiful homes and thought we had everything we could possibly want – supposedly living the Baby Boomer dream.

Another thing we had in common was that we'd both had our share of shocks from being hit hard with life's unexpected but pivotal events. Maybe you can relate to our experience.

It's a shock to find yourself separated and going through divorce, having spent years working at what you thought was the perfect relationship. The love that you thought was for a lifetime gets overpowered by negotiations to divide up assets.

It's a shock that the happiness and fulfilment brought by achieving financial success can be so short-lived.

It's a shock to realize that having strived to be the best at everything, you are not invincible to disease and ill health. This especially hit home when Sue was diagnosed with breast cancer and Penny with Hashimoto's disease.

We were both devastated that our families were being split up and had vowed never to put our children through what we had gone through as children when our parents divorced. The guilt and shame over what seemed like personal failure was taking its toll. For each of us, the past was influencing our approach to life, and we both found ourselves off track and out of sync. In our parallel lives, we felt anxious, overwhelmed, stressed and burnt out.

The glue of love in our marriages, as well the financial success we'd shared with our husbands, was all coming unstuck, and we were falling apart. People we had counted on were turning away from us. We each found ourselves feeling adrift, powerless and unsafe, not knowing what the future would bring. We were both wondering whether we would be able to cope on our own.

Deep down inside, we had a knowing that there was a way forward out of our powerlessness to effect change. A turning point came when we realized that we had been looking for happiness in the wrong place. We'd had apparent success on the outside – family, material, financial, social – but this was no longer making us happy nor was it fulfilling us. In our marriages, we had looked to our partners for love and security, but ended up blaming them and feeling disappointed when expectations weren't met.

After all of this we realized that we had a desire to find a better way of living. We wanted to feel alive and to light up our lives again. We were acutely aware of our pain, loss and past hurt and were determined to find a way of getting beyond it.

THE SEARCH BEGINS

We started attending courses and reading books, learning everything we could about improving our self-awareness and identifying what was taking us off track. We embarked on a journey of exploration to find whatever we needed to successfully navigate challenges and prepare ourselves for the opportunities ahead.

In our search we travelled far and wide through India, Burma, Thailand, Nepal, Bhutan, Japan, Australia, the United States, Peru, Brazil and Costa Rica, gaining new insights and perspectives.

We had a lot of fun and met some weird and wonderful characters. Mother Martha in California had us crawling through a metaphorical birth canal to get in touch with stored memories and emotions. Psychological Peter in London helped us to unravel our past and our conditioning. These new encounters made us realize that we both had limiting beliefs from our childhood, such as *I am not good enough* or *I'm not loveable*. Through Life-Force Lily in India, we shook our Kundalini to remember our natural sexual energy and how to have healthy relationships. In Costa Rica, Ecstatic Erica danced us into our bodies, Blissful Brian taught us meditation, and Massage Mary smoothed our bodily knots and wrinkles away. We found ourselves tapping our meridians, hugging trees, walking on hot coals and leaping from great heights, all in the name of self-development.

Between us, during this stage of our journey, we left no enlightenment stone unturned. We tried out over 60 different methods of self-development with as many different teachers. We had plummeted to the darkest depths and faced our deepest fears, and like the mythical Phoenix, we had risen from those ashes and found the light – or so we thought.

Had we *really* reached nirvana? No, but instead something different happened. Having done the work with so many different gurus, we came to the conclusion that no one had the complete answer, and furthermore, we weren't drawn to blindly devote ourselves to any of them.

Please don't get the wrong idea here – all of our teachers were valuable in their own right, and we respect their different doctrines. But while we felt a lot happier, there remained an underlying frustration. We soon realized that our frustration was with ourselves for giving our power away to others. As a result of this self-development journey, we realized that we needed to stop looking on the outside and start looking inside ourselves. It was time to start believing in our own power!

It had become clear that no one was going to do this for us and actually we had always had everything we needed to get through this within us.

Piece by piece as we travelled from place to place and teacher to teacher the puzzle appeared to have finally come together, revealing that we were more powerful in our own right than we had realized.

However, when we started to put this into practice, we found that there were still some things missing. We discovered that it wasn't easy to apply what we had learned to our everyday lives.

Maybe you have been there yourself.

We set an intention to find the secret to the missing pieces and trusted that the answers would turn up. We wanted to find a way to explain what we had learned in clear, everyday language, rather than what is often perceived as mumbo jumbo from alternative traditions. We wanted to make the wisdom more accessible for ourselves and ultimately for other people, which meant we would need to get beyond resistance to dogma and specific religious connotations.

Synchronistically, while attending a coaching conference at which she was speaking, we met an amazing woman who opened our eyes to the world of energy. Zinging Zelda was working at the leading edge of personal development. From her, we learned about energy and how, if we manage our own personal energy, life enters a state of ease and flow. In that state, we can effortlessly manifest what it is we want to experience in our lives.

At the same time, everywhere we turned we kept bumping into people who were talking about neuroscience and how the brain affects behaviour. A new, cutting-edge science was providing us with the evidence to support what we had learned and the language to explain the relationship between the mind, body and the external world.

The missing pieces were finally in place, and we were ready to road test our new approach. We blended together the most effective elements from different approaches into a simple, easy-to-apply practice that we could use every day to be fully present, access a state of flow at will, get into 'the zone' and feel at our very best. Applying this simple practice enabled Sue to smash her advanced coaching assessment, despite being the least experienced person on the programme. It helped Penny to navigate a devastating financial fraud and discover that money was not the source of her happiness.

Through these experiences, we realized that we didn't need to go on a week's silent retreat, fast or sit for hours meditating to attain a powerful, natural state of being. We realized that such a state is always available when you know how to access it, a process that we found was as simple and easy as turning on a light switch.

Full power, we now knew, is always available if only we can find and use the switch to access it.

Stunned by the impact this method was having on the big challenges we were facing, as well as transforming our everyday lives, we started to have a vision as to how we could share it with others and make a real difference in their lives too.

This vision was translated into our mission to shortcut for others the journey we had been on. We were passionate about blending together our self-development learning experience with our coaching and facilitation skills to make it easy and accessible for anyone to get into what we call the 'zone of connection', or ZOC as we'll call it from now on, and to fully connect with themselves, others and the world around them. We knew that this would enable people to access their true power and live their lives to the fullest.

Since 2008, our work has taken on a life of its own. We shared our transformational approach with many hundreds of people from every walk of life, individually, in workshops, at retreats, conferences, in master classes, and in train-the-trainer and coaching programmes.

We shared with others that when disconnected from our true selves, we are in a *default operating system* that automatically and unconsciously reacts to events, causing stress, anxiety and overwhelm. In that state, it's difficult to be present in relationships and, due to a limited perspective, we can realize only a fraction of our potential. We are stuck in our past pain, feeling powerless and unable to make vital changes.

However, we can choose to shift out of this default operating system to one of full connection accessed through the ZOC. What we have discovered is that a *full-connection operating system* has been there all the time, and we can all easily access it. It is this full-connection operating system that the great masters and ancient wisdom traditions point to – a beautiful, powerful state that is now available to everyone.

HOW THIS IS RELEVANT FOR YOU

These are challenging times. At a collective level, we're faced with huge challenges: climate change, political upheaval, social unrest and economic inequality. These are sometimes referred to as VUCA times – *volatile, uncertain, complex* and *ambiguous* – an acronym coined by the US military in 1990s.

In our personal lives, we also face constant change and the challenges and anxieties of modern-day living, such as the need to make a living and find time to do the things that feel meaningful in the midst of information overload.

There may be times when you feel as if you are on autopilot and not in control of your own life, that events are happening to you, that are out of your control. Possibly you feel overwhelmed by life, not coping or enjoying what you are doing or have, feeling stressed and anxious. Perhaps you are disconnected and your relationships are suffering as a result. It could be that you feel stuck and unable to deal with change and the challenges life is throwing at you. Or maybe you just want to explore other possibilities.

Imagine a life where no matter what happens, you are able not only to survive, but to thrive. You are able to consciously choose how your life unfolds. You are in the zone where life is flowing, making you feel happy and giving you a sense of satisfaction and fulfilment as your very presence makes a difference to the lives of those around you. You are in your true power and have a deep sense of wellbeing.

How do you get from the place of stress, overwhelm, off track and being on autopilot to a place of inner peace, where you are in the ZOC and consciously creating the life you desire?

We asked ourselves that very question. Our answer was to develop a technique we call the Connection Practice, a routine that consistently gives people the easiest access to a state of full connection. In this fully connected, whole-being state, you have shifted from your default operating system, which automatically reacts to events, to a new operating system. This allows you to interrupt your habitual negative thoughts and patterns of behaviour, freeing yourself from the prison of your mind. Your body chemistry is optimal, giving you a sense of health and wellbeing. You sense that everything is just right; you are connected to your true power. You are calm and centred yet feel vibrantly alive.

With regular training, the Connection Practice teaches your brain to remain in this new operating system. It establishes a new way of being that will endure and has an impact on your day-to-day life, something you can always turn to. It gives you the power to reprogram yourself, thus changing the course of your life to a more positive, abundant one that you control.

This is actually a natural way of being for all of us; it has been in the background all the time, but the majority of us either don't know that it exists or how to access it. Now we have created an easy way for you to reach it. The Connection Practice will short-circuit your journey and take you straight to accessing this zone and your own full power every day. Integrating this simple routine into your life will help you to deal with the challenges life throws at you. It will enable you to grow, thrive, become more of who you are and realize more of your potential. It is the secret to transforming your life and empowers you to get to where you want to be.

We can use the Connection Practice to shift beyond the small, mistaken, ego-based identity that has us operating on autopilot with increasing stress and burnout, to a bigger, more expansive perspective that sees the potential in every situation. This expanded consciousness represents the next level of development for human beings, one that we can all be a part of. It is a new operating system for our daily lives enabling us to function wisely, effectively and joyfully in the world today to meet these challenges. Such an expanded operating system is not just for a few enlightened gurus, but rather it's available to everyone who integrates the Connection Practice into their life.

Keeping your operating system up to date is vital for health and wellbeing in today's rapidly changing world. So, if you want to stay ahead of the game and be the best version of yourself, you are in the right place!

WHY THE CONNECTION PRACTICE
AND WHY THIS BOOK

Our intention in this book is to share our approach with you and inspire you to put it into practice. Then you, too, can unlock your true power and potential and have a better quality of life every day and the best chance to feel happy and thrive. This life-transforming practice is easy for anyone to master and only takes a few minutes when you make it your own.

In this book, we will share with you the seven fundamentals for living in the ZOC, which all have the Connection Practice at their core:

1. **C**onnect up – how to shift from autopilot to living in the zone, in your true full power
2. **O**pen Up – how to put in place the mindset that supports you to open to your true power
3. **N**ourish your real self – how to connect with and live from your real self
4. **N**urture relationships – how to create fully connected *real*-ationships
5. **E**xpress yourself fully – how to use true communication to fully connect with others
6. **C**reate an abundant life – how to connect with your ability to create and manifest the life you want to live
7. **T**ransform your life – how to connect with energy and allow it to flow to transform your life

What you learn in this book will help you with:

- Anxiety and stress
- Overcoming fear barriers
- Breaking negative patterns
- Overall health and wellbeing

It will also help you with:
- Feeling happy, calm, peaceful, joyful and blissful
- Confidence and resilience
- Being present and in flow in the moment
- Being authentic
- Your relationship with yourself and others
- Seeing potential and opportunity
- Manifesting abundance
- Feeling fulfilled
- Being in your full true power

Integrate the teachings and practices from this book into your life, and you will find that you start to operate from your highest self. You will feel at your best and be able to manage how you influence others. In essence, you'll feel relaxed and calm, confident, with a sense of wellbeing and peace, giving you the best opportunity to manifest happiness and abundance, to have a far-reaching positive impact on yourself, others and the world around you.

Our intention is to share the practice and benefits of this work with all those who are interested and give the guidance needed to use it easily in everyday life. Our aim is to make this approach accessible to everyone in both its practice and language.

Robbie, a coach who attended our masterclass, told us he was unable to be authentic and so wasn't having the impact he knew he was capable of with his clients. Learning the Connection Practice and applying it in his own life was transformational for him: "It is one of the single things that has made the biggest difference to my life. It has helped me in so many ways." Specifically, he told us how he was enabled to: overcome limiting beliefs; spend more time in the here and now; spend more time in a feeling place; feel satisfied with his work; be with his clients, fully present and ready for them; get into the zone and flow at will and spend more time there.

This is an example of how using the Connection Practice to access the ZOC can change your life.

So, whether, like us, you have tried many techniques and are a long way through this journey, or you are a newcomer and looking for a fresh way to get started, the Connection Practice will accelerate your journey, and add to what you've already done. It gives you the final piece of the puzzle: how to live in your full power every day.

Today many more people are receptive to practices such as mindfulness, appreciating the benefits they bring. This has created a readiness for our approach, which goes beyond mindfulness. We know the time has come to share this gift more widely.

HOW TO USE THIS BOOK

The Zone of Connection is a combination of text and experiential exercises. We recommend that you download the audio version for all of the exercises, so you can easily access them as you go through the book. The audios can be found using the link below or scanning the QR code.

The exercises build on each other, so it is advisable to follow them in the order that they appear in the book.

The exercises must be experienced and felt to have an impact; we know that reading them alone will not create any shift in you.

We would also suggest that you get yourself a beautiful journal to write in as you work through the exercises. Or, if you prefer, you can create an electronic journal.

However you choose to start your journey toward a deeper connection to yourself and to life, we welcome you and thank you for coming along with us. We are honoured to have the opportunity to share *The Zone of Connection* with you.

Download the audio versions of the exercises by following the link below or scanning the QR code:

thezoneofconnection.com/downloads

CHAPTER 2

The Scientific Context

"We think we live in a three-dimensional material world, whereas we actually live in a multi-dimensional energetic world. The reason we are unaware of this larger reality is that we have filtered it out. Further progress in the evolution of consciousness requires us to stop filtering our awareness and start expanding our awareness."

Richard Barrett

Does science have the answers?

We were surprised by what we found. What if you knew that:

- You have more than one brain
- You spend most of your life on autopilot
- Your thoughts can make you stressed and ill
- You can flip a switch to change your brain's operating system and change your state

In this new operating system you can:

- Access all of your brain for maximum brainpower
- Make your new power sustainable by rewiring your brain
- Alter your brainwaves and chemicals to feel good
- Influence the state of other people in only a few minutes
- Use your innate abilities to access a quantum level of intelligence
- Be in your full, true power, accessing flow and the zone instantly
- Use intentions to create your life

There has been a wealth of research and information written in recent years about how human beings function, from both a scientific and psychological perspective. In this chapter, we offer a synopsis of the latest understanding that underpins our approach in *The Zone of Connection* and helps to explain what it is and why it works. Our intention is to provide a map of the terrain from our own understanding and experience that you can recognize and relate to on your journey.

THE JOURNEY OF A HUMAN BEING

Scientists believe that in the beginning there was a Big Bang. This amazing cosmological event took place about 13.8 billion years ago. At that moment, our physical universe came into being out of the universal energy field. This energy field is the container for everything that exists, and that includes us.

Quantum science, which explains the nature and behaviour of matter and energy, has discovered fundamental properties that apply to the energy world. Everything is energy and, as such, is wave-like and vibrates at different frequencies. Because there is no time and space in this energy world, everything is interconnected. There is no limitation in this universal energy field, and everything is possible. We create our reality through our thoughts and where we focus our attention. In this way, we transform 'thought energy' into matter in the material, physical world in which we live. Everything that has been created by human beings in our world was once just a thought in someone's mind.

A similarly amazing Small Bang happens when we are conceived, as a sperm and egg come together to create an embryo. At that early stage, the embryo is more a part of the energy (explained later in this chapter in the Quantum Science section) than the physical world and, as such, it is an individual part of the universal energy field, referred to as our 'energetic self'.

THE PSYCHOLOGICAL AND ENERGETIC STAGES OF DEVELOPMENT

The energetic self grows and develops in stages (for more on this, see Richard Barrett's book, *A New Psychology of Human Well-Being*. There's a list of all the books referred to at the back of this book, with their publication details).

Once you are born, your psychological and energetic development follow parallel journeys.

Survival (0–2 years)

We all begin as a ball of energy in our mother's womb. When we have been in the womb for about three months, our *reptilian brain* starts to function. It's called the reptilian brain because it's been with us since the era of the dinosaurs, about 100 million years.

During this early stage, from our time in the womb until we are about two years old, our instinctive focus is staying alive. The reptilian brain plays a big part in that effort, as it exists solely for our physical survival.

Our belief system starts to form even at this early stage. When all of the physical survival needs of an infant are met by their caretakers, they form the subconscious belief that the world is safe and people can be trusted. If, on the other hand, the infant is neglected, put in danger, hurt, not fed, not cuddled or not kept clean, their subconscious belief is that the world is not safe. These beliefs stay with us into our adult life.

Babies who are born prematurely experience the shock of being brought into the world before they are ready. This can create a hypervigilance, which can lead to ADHD (attention deficit hyper-activity disorder).

Robert Keegan, professor at Harvard School of Education, said that during this stage of development, we are transitioning from the energy field to learning how to be in a body with all the limi-tations of being in the physical world.

Relationships (2–7 years)

Between the ages of two and seven, we learn to walk and talk, and we start to build relationships. During this period, the portion of the brain that forms the subconscious mind and controls emotions, memories and stimulation, better known as the *limbic brain*, starts to develop. Our needs at this stage of development are to feel love and belonging from those we are close to, as well as to keep our body safe from harm. If these needs are fulfilled, it gives us a sense of physical and emotional safety.

During this time our brain continues to develop and like a sponge it absorbs the beliefs of those around us, which eventually become hardwired in our long-term memory. By the age of seven, all of the hardwired subconscious beliefs that later influence our future decisions and behaviours are in place.

Not receiving the attention we need at this stage, feeling unloved, not accepted, not protected and as if we don't belong will result in us developing the subconscious belief that we are not loveable. This stays with us and, as we grow older, we may become needy, searching for love. If, on the other hand, we do feel loved, accepted and safe, we are able to form committed relationships as adults.

For example, children who lose a parent at this stage of development are likely to grow up with a fear of abandonment that plays out in their adult life. Or children who experience sibling rivalry will set patterns of behaviour that unconsciously play out in their relationships going forward.

Children at this stage are often open-minded and innocent, still able to access their energetic nature. This gives them a freedom to play and experience spontaneity and joy. But our connection to our energetic self gradually becomes blocked by our education and social belief systems. George Land's landmark study, reported in *Breakpoint and Beyond,* explored the changing levels of creativity of a cohort of 1,600 children as they grew into adulthood. He found that 98% of children in the 3–5 age group had genius-level creativity, but only 32% had that same level at aged 8–10. Another five years later, for the 13–15 age group, the level of creativity fell to 10%. George Land used the same tests in a study of 200,000 people aged 25 and over and only 2% were found to be at the genius level for creativity.

Self-esteem (8–24 years)

Around the age of seven or eight, the *neocortex brain*, which is responsible for the rational mind, becomes functional. From the age of eight, we start to explore the world beyond the confines of our home. The brain continues growing until the age of 25. This phase is very much focused on 'I', as the adolescent explores the boundaries of who they are. Sexuality characteristics and behaviours also develop around this stage.

We can no longer rely solely on our parents for personal safety as we move through this stage, so relationships with peer groups and other influential people in our lives, such as teachers, become important.

We try to get recognition and respect not only from our parents, but also from these other groups outside of the home by exploring our identity, learning what our gifts and talents are, and developing our strengths. Feeling accepted by others gives us a sense of physical and emotional security and self-worth.

If your efforts are not appreciated, and you don't get positive feedback from parents, teachers and those important to you, you may develop a belief that you are not good enough and have a low sense of self-esteem. This will remain with you through your life, and as an adult you may not feel worthy or you may become competitive and seek status and power to boost your self-importance. In addition, this may result in developing a fear of failure, which could either drive you or lead to you avoiding challenges.

In order to continue our development beyond these first three stages, we naturally start an inner journey of moving beyond our fears, and this starts from around the age of 25.

Transformation (25–39 years)

As we reach our mid-20s, we want to break away and become independent. We want to find a way of being self-sufficient so that we have the freedom and autonomy we desire. We want to find our authentic self, be able to live according to our own values, and be responsible and accountable for our life. This is a transformational stage where we have a chance to start the inner journey and connect more deeply again to the energetic part of our self.

Sometimes this breaking away and becoming autonomous can bring up a lot of fear. If we have not had our needs met at the first three stages of development, we may find ourselves stuck in the earlier self-esteem, relationship and survival levels. For us, we found ourselves striving to be successful in our careers during this stage in order to ensure we were financially independent and prove that we were good enough.

By using techniques such as the Connection Practice, you become the observer or witness of your inner landscape, which helps you to master this stage and get back in touch with your energetic self. You can become aware of your emotions, thoughts and fears, and bring them to conscious awareness. Then you can let go of them, freeing yourself to move on to the subsequent stages during which you have the opportunity to start the process of reconnecting with all of yourself.

Self-expression (40–49 years)

This stage is all about a continuation of our inner growth as we discover and connect to what our beliefs and talents are, what our purpose is and who we really are in our true nature – an energetic being. At this stage we start to look for more meaning in our lives.

At a deep level we have always known what our life purpose is, but at this stage of development we are ready to bring this to conscious awareness. This requires deep reflection on questions such as:

- What is it people often ask you to help them with?
- What have you learned/what gifts and talents have you used to overcome the challenges you have experienced in your life so far?
- What are the common threads that link moments when you have felt a deep sense of satisfaction?

Some people successfully align with their life purpose and feel a great sense of fulfilment and happiness. However, many get stuck here, maybe with a mid-life crisis or in a job that supports the lifestyle they want for their family, but doesn't align with their life purpose. This stops them from fully expressing themselves. It may cause them to feel that their life lacks meaning and ultimately can lead to dis-ease and physical illness in the body, which happened to both Sue and Penny, as we dealt with our health issues. We also had a mid-life crisis on our hands, as we both got divorced during this stage.

Making a difference (50–59 years)

At this stage of our lives, if we have done the inner work of understanding who we are and connecting with our life purpose, we can then start to connect with others who share our passion and purpose, and use our talents to make an even bigger difference.

It is easy to become overfocused on your own purpose and the contribution you can make as an individual. But in our experience of collaborating with others when sharing the Connection Practice, we know that this not only expands the number of lives we touch, but it is also very fulfilling.

As you progress through this stage, you start to realize your full potential and by sharing your wisdom, compassion and higher levels of intelligence contribute to the common good. If you are fully aligned with your purpose, you will feel that your life is in flow and that synchronicities occur to enable you to make your difference.

Service (60+)

This final stage of development is about selfless service to your community. It is about making a contribution. It doesn't matter how big or small your contribution is, what is important is to know that your life has a purpose.

By deepening your connection to your true self through reflection and practices such as meditation, you will experience a sense of meaning and levels of fulfilment and wellbeing you have never experienced before. You will see how connected we all are and how by serving others you are serving the greater good.

The table setting out the psychological and energetic stages of development sums up the broad stages of development, the approximate age at which you might experience them, and the focus or motivation as you journey through each stage. It also points out the concerns or limiting beliefs that can hold you back at each stage.

The psychological and energetic stages of development

—

Stage of psychological development	Approximate age range	Level of consciousness	Motivation	Associated limiting beliefs/ concerns
Serving	60+	Service	Need for selfless service	I feel lonely. I have nothing to offer my community
Integrating	50-59	Making a difference	Need to make a difference	I feel isolated. I have nothing in common with the people around me
Self-actualizing	40-49	Self-expression	Find meaning and purpose	I feel my life is meaningless. I don't know what my gifts and talents are
Individuating	25-39	Transformation	Need for freedom and autonomy	I feel trapped. I can't find a way to discover who I am
Differentiating	8-24	Self-esteem	Need for recognition and respect	I don't feel seen or heard. I don't belong anywhere. I am not enough
Conforming	2-7	Relationships	Need for love and belonging	I feel unsafe and unprotected. I am unlovable
Surviving	0-2	Survival	Need for physiological survival	I feel vulnerable, I do not have what I need to survive

CAUSES OF DISCONNECTION

During the first three stages of psychological and energetic development, we gradually disconnect from our energetic self. What follows is the exploration of three things that keep us disconnected and stuck in these ego-based stages of survival, relationships and self-esteem.

Limiting beliefs

As we have already said, by the age of seven all of the hard-wired beliefs that later influence our choices and behaviours are in place. As adults, most of us have a seven-year-old running our lives!

But the beliefs you take on as a child – through the influence of those around you – may not be relevant to you when you become an adult.

The core limiting beliefs that can result from our first three stages of development (survival, relationships and self-esteem) include: I don't have enough, I am not loveable, and I am not good enough.

These unconscious beliefs based on past fears hold you back later in life and cause you to stay in your comfort zone, preventing you from growing and realizing your potential.

Automatic patterns

Between the ages of two and seven, you learn that there are rules and ways of behaving that your family expects you to adhere to, and so you learn to fit in largely by imitating your caregivers. You do this using your *mirror neurons*, brain cells that allow you to feel empathy with others and copy behavioural patterns. We'll explore the value of mirror neurons in more detail later in this chapter.

Having clear rules and boundaries helps you to feel phys-ically and emotionally safe. However, complications arise if, in order to get your needs met, you believe that you need to behave in a certain way. These behavioural patterns then become embedded in your unconscious mind and continue to play out throughout your life.

Some of the common patterns that show up are:

- Needing to be perfect
- Needing to be liked so you tend to want to please others and put them first
- Trying hard to prove that you are good enough
- Avoiding emotions and situations that make you feel uncomfortable or unsafe
- Not believing there is enough – scarcity mentality

Blocked emotions

As human beings, we are unique in the animal kingdom by having feelings and corresponding emotions. An emotion is a form of energy signalling us to respond. In the Western world, we have often been taught to repress, suppress and judge emotions as good or bad, but what we know now is that emotions are just energy designed to give us a message and then move through us.

When you suppress emotions they get blocked in the body, forming tension and imbalance. Suppression also robs your body of energy that is needed to function and affects your immune system. All of which, in turn, can eventually lead to disease and illness, as explored in the science of psycho-neuro-immunology by Candace Pert, PhD and Bruce Lipton, PhD.

As you go through life, blocked emotions can be triggered when you experience external events that are negative and that unconsciously remind you of the original event when the emotions became blocked. These may cause you to relive experiences from your past and react in a way that is not appropriate to the current situation. Therefore, this repetition keeps you stuck in the past and trapped in fear-based defensive behaviours. You may think that your reactions are caused by someone or something outside of you, but really it is your own patterns, attitudes and feelings about what you say and do that trigger your emotional reactions.

Have you ever felt that your reaction has been disproportionate to that required by a situation? Maybe you have felt the loss of a loved one or a relationship, and been surprised how sadness and grief can come up unexpectedly in other unrelated situations.

This shows it is the unfinished business from your past and a whole life of false beliefs stored in your subconscious mind that cause an unconscious reaction to a present situation, and not the one you would consciously choose. This is where you are on auto-pilot, and your default operating system is in control. You have a reaction based on your misunderstandings and false information. To take this analogy further, we could say that the limiting beliefs, automatic patterns and blocked emotions are like bugs and viruses that limit the effectiveness of the system.

An important point to keep in mind is that negative beliefs and emotions are destructive, cause disease, illness and premature ageing, while positive emotions foster health, wellbeing and happiness. The negative influences are set deep in your subconscious, and once formed they continue to repeat themselves throughout your life unless you decide to create a new path. As your reality is shaped by your experiences and expectations, when you believe in something or a vision, this is what you will attract and create in your life.

THE NEW SCIENCE

New scientific findings give us an understanding of what we do naturally when being our best and how to go beyond the unconscious, built-in patterns that limit us. Such findings can also be used to help demystify the energy world by providing the explanations that we require.

New Science is the theoretical context behind our approach and offers empirical understanding and evidence. We are not claiming to be masters of New Science; however, it helps us to give a scientific grounding for how transformation takes place practically.

Two fields of New Science are *neuroscience* and *quantum science*, made more accessible to people through the writings and teachings of Dr Joe Dispenza, Dr Daniel Siegel and Dr Brian Cox. Their work and the work of many others has taken the mystery out of our understanding about how we and the universe function.

Neuroscience

What is neuroscience? It's the study of the nervous system and the brain. It helps us to understand the actual physiological functioning of our brains, and how it affects our mind and body's performance and our whole energy system.

Over the last ten years, the neuroscience field has made enormous progress. Today, this progressive field provides us with the opportunity not only to understand more clearly how we work, but also to do something about it.

Before we delve in detail into neuroscience, it is worth noting that the words *brain* and *mind* are often used interchangeably. In this book, when we use the word *brain* we are referring to the physical organ consisting of neurons, synapses and electrical impulses. We use the word *mind*, on the other hand, to refer to the energetic instrument that controls the functions of the body.

As Dr Daniel Siegel of the Mindsight Institute explains, "The mind is an embodied and relational process that regulates the flow of energy and information."

We can learn to use the mind to access flows of energy and information, and so be at our best in life.

Through the studies of neuroscience, it has been shown that our brain is not only located in the skull. In fact, we have three brains: the *head brain* with 100 billion neurons, the *heart brain* with 120 million neurons and the *gut brain* with 500 million neurons. The heart generates an electromagnetic field 5,000 times more powerful than that of the head brain (Institute of Heart Math).

The reality of this three-part brain is reflected in our language and behaviour. For example, you may put your hand on your heart and say something is 'heartfelt', or say you have a 'gut feeling' or someone is 'gutsy and courageous' (see Grant Soosalu and Marvin Oka, *mBraining: Using Your Multiple Brains to Do Cool Stuff*).

You can use each of these three brains alone, or connect to all three for much more powerful results. For instance, when you are only in your head brain, you are overwhelmed by past experiences or thoughts of the future. But, when you are connected with your three brains, you are more present in the moment, more aware of your senses, and you can use your innate abilities more fully. When these three brains work together, you enter into autonomic balance and coherence, an optimal state of neurological balance where you can access a state of flow. You have a more accurate sense of reality.

New Science: the three brains

—

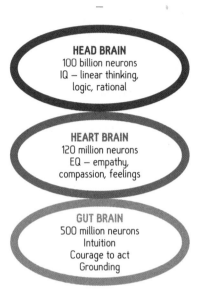

Unfortunately, we are not taught about this and how to take advantage of *neuroplasticity* to rewire our brains and update our beliefs.

Now let's explore where your mind's functions are in the brain.

The *conscious mind* is in the *neocortex* part of the brain, where we make all of our logical and rational decisions. This contains our short-term memories.

The *subconscious mind* is in the *limbic brain*, which develops between the ages of two and seven. This is where our emotional memories are stored and can be accessed by hypnosis.

The *unconscious mind* is in the *reptilian brain* that develops by the age of two. It runs all of the automatic programs, such as breathing, and stores memories, patterns or imprints of which we are not aware. This runs on autopilot and controls our default operating system.

The three levels of mind function in the brain

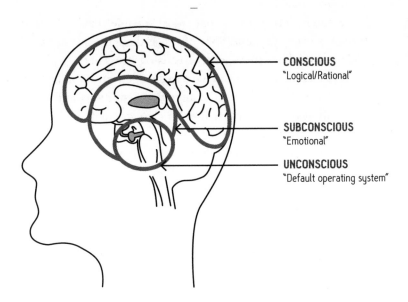

CONSCIOUS
"Logical/Rational"

SUBCONSCIOUS
"Emotional"

UNCONSCIOUS
"Default operating system"

The unconscious mind is not some black hole of unacceptable impulses waiting to trip you up. It takes in and stores information from our five senses and has a much greater capacity for storing information than the conscious mind. In her book *Charismatic to the Core*, Nikki Owen refers to the unconscious mind as "a goldmine of resources" and a source of "untapped wisdom".

At the same time, the unconscious mind is the source of hidden beliefs, fears and attitudes that interfere with your everyday life. Most forms of psychotherapy aim to bring into conscious awareness many of these hidden hindrances, so that you can examine them and choose how to deal with them.

This part of the mind is inaccessible to the conscious mind, but affects behaviour and emotions. Everything has a function, and we experience emotions and feelings as a call to take action. Hence, our decisions are often made unconsciously at an emotional level.

Research has shown that most people have 100,000 thoughts every day, and 95% of those thoughts are negative and many of them are repetitive, causing stress in the body. To change such behaviour, you have to change your thoughts and beliefs, which in turn will change your emotions and energetic vibration. We explore how to change our thoughts and beliefs in Chapter 4, Opening Up.

The brain has an overarching organizing principle, which is to classify the world into things that either hurt you or help you to stay alive. This is concerned with minimizing danger or maximizing reward. There are two possible states that result from this: the *away state* and the *toward state*.

In the *away state*, you are closed down, have a narrow focus on the danger or threat, and feel negative due to a lack of the brain chemical *dopamine*. In this state, the reptilian brain is the control centre for your survival instinct, the 'fight or flight' response. For our ancestors, fight or flight was the response to seeing a sabre-toothed tiger, but today we create psychological fear in response to a perceived, not real, threat. When fight/flight/freeze reactions are activated, your default operating system shuts down your prefrontal cortex, which would otherwise use a lot of energy, and creates an 'amygdala hijack', causing a loss of brainpower. Thinking is then impaired, drastically affecting your ability to function well.

When you are stressed, anxious or fearful, blood is sent to the parts of the body you need for survival – muscles, heart, lungs, adrenal glands – and the brain and body is flooded with *cortisol* and *adrenaline*, the stress hormones. In reality, the body can only cope with short periods of this type of reaction. However, in today's world of chaos and continual change, there is instead a constant amygdala hijack at a low level, with the related psychological and physiological effects.

This can create both physical and mental health problems as the immune system becomes compromised.

How often do you feel the negative effects of the stress response kicking in and taking away your true power?

On the other hand, the *toward state* of the brain is about reward. When you are in this state you feel valued, open to change and have a bigger perspective on life – you are more creative and can think clearly. The 'feel good' brain chemicals are prevalent when you are in the reward state; these are *dopamine, oxytocin,* and *serotonin.* When you feel connection, for example hugging someone, watching a romantic film or stroking an animal, your hypothalamus produces and releases oxytocin. Activities such as smiling and exercising influence your body's production and release of dopamine, also from the hypothalamus. Serotonin, which is produced in the gut brain, contributes to wellbeing and happiness. The natural production of serotonin can be interrupted or influenced by stress and poor diet. Drug habits can create artificial highs of serotonin and dopamine that the body then tries to counteract, throwing itself out of balance and creating addiction.

Due to its *neuroplasticity*, our brain is amazingly adaptable. Its capacity to continue to grow and rewire itself enables us to learn and change continuously throughout our lives. Neuroplasticity enables you to literally evolve yourself to higher orders of functioning. In order to maintain the neuroplasticity of your brain, you can make a conscious choice to try new ways of thinking and try things that provide you with new insights. This is discussed in more detail in Chapter 4, Opening Up.

An example of how this is possible comes from Sue's experience of having chemotherapy, after which she had what is known as 'chemo-brain'. When someone she knew called on the phone, she experienced a time lapse and couldn't remember who they were. It felt as though there was a trip wire slowly connecting to her memory of who this person was. Over time, through consciously working with this, neuroplasticity restored her memory's capacity to remember people.

Let's explore some more examples of neuroplasticity.

A study done by Richard Davidson, a professor of psychology and psychiatry at the University of Wisconsin, showed that when Buddhist monks experienced bliss as they entered into deep meditation, the left prefrontal lobe of their brains showed increased electrical activity. The findings in this study suggested that bliss or happiness is not just a vague feeling but also a physical state of the brain. More importantly, this physical state can be induced deliberately. Davidson refers to this as "making a left shift".

Another study supported the function of neuroplasticity by showing that the practice of mindfulness and meditation increases the size of the part of the brain related to feelings of happiness.

Mindful practices have other positive effects as well. Research studies conducted by the department of psychiatry at Oxford University showed that in a course on practising mindfulness among participants, there was a 58% reduction in anxiety, a 40% reduction in stress and a 57% reduction in depression.

Another study by the School of Psychology at the University of Surrey found that people completing a mindfulness course showed a 40% decrease in rumination, a 26% reduction in chronic fatigue and a 33% improvement in sleep quality.

Mindfulness practice and meditation also have a proven effect on our mental functions, such as:

- Emotion balancing
- Fear reduction
- Empathy
- Intuition
- Response flexibility
- Insight and self-awareness
- Focus

The Connection Practice goes beyond mindfulness and offers an alternative to our default autopilot operating system. We call this alternative operating system *full connection living*. Operating in this state regularly grows new neural connections and, as a result of neuroplasticity, rewires your brain.

BRAINWAVE FREQUENCIES: DAILY ACTIVITIES AND EFFECT ON BRAINWAVES

Your brain has the ability to operate at five different brainwave frequencies. These frequencies are produced by the electrical pulses from masses of neurons communicating with each other. Your brain can change frequency at different times during the day according to what you are doing and feeling. The different brainwave frequencies heavily influence your state because each frequency puts you into a different state of consciousness.

Let's look at each of the five major brain frequencies and then explore how to use this understanding to improve your life.

Brainwave frequencies

There are five main brainwave frequencies as shown in the table: gamma, beta, alpha, theta and delta. These are measured in cycles per second (measured in hertz [Hz]). The higher the frequency, the greater the activity and, in general, the emotions that you feel will be more volatile.

The five main brainwave frequencies

—

Brainwave frequency	Hz (cycles per second)	State	Brain/mind	Benefits	Drawbacks
Gamma	40–100	Bursts of insight, brief and intensive	High-level information processing	Helps us to grow new neural connections	Too much can cause anxiety
Beta	14–40	Active, alert, externally focused	Logical. Default frequency	Concen-tration, alertness	Can become stimulus junkie, difficult to focus, negative inner voice
Alpha	7.5–14	Deep relaxation, meditation, more of an inner focus	Bridge between subconscious and conscious mind	Creativity, imagination	No drawbacks
Theta	4–7.5	Very deep relaxation e.g., hypnosis, meditation, REM sleep. Body asleep, mind awake	Subconscious mind	Instan-taneous change can take place	No drawbacks
Delta	0–4	Deep dreamless sleep, totally detached, transcendental meditation	Unconscious bodily functions	Healing occurs	No drawbacks

Here the five brainwave frequencies are described further:

- **Gamma waves** have the fastest frequency at 40–100 Hz. This range is the most recently discovered and while little is known about this state of mind, initial research shows gamma waves are associated with bursts of insight, high-level information processing tasks, and cognitive functioning such as learning, memory and information processing. Your brain does not operate in the gamma frequency region very often; it is generally a brief but intense experience. Too much can cause anxiety and high arousal, too little can cause learning disabilities. One extraordinary discovery is that when neurons fire together they grow new connections and wire together, making new neural structures; it is the gamma waves that enable this to happen.

- **Beta waves** have a frequency of 14–40 Hz. This is the most common frequency that your brain operates in. It definitely has its benefits, but also has serious drawbacks as our 'default' frequency. People in beta are prone to be stimulus junkies and have a difficult time focusing. When you hear that little negative voice inside you, that is the dark side of beta coming out.

- **Alpha waves** have a frequency of 7.5–14 Hz. When your brain operates in the alpha region, you will find that your inner world of imagination tends to be more real than the outer physical world. In this state, although you will still be able to sense the outer world, you pay more attention to the inner world. Have you ever been in the shower and been struck by a brilliant solution to a problem that's been nagging you for a long time?

  That's the benefit of the alpha frequency. The alpha frequency is great because it is when you are most creative. People who spend more time in alpha tend to be more relaxed, focused and imaginative than people who spend most of their time in beta.

- **Theta waves** have a frequency of 4–7.5 Hz. If you relax a little bit more and your breathing starts to change, you will slip into theta brainwave patterns. That is when your body is asleep and your mind is awake. It is a state of very deep relaxation as used in hypnosis and occurs during meditation and rapid eye movement (REM) sleep. Theta brainwaves can be considered to be from the subconscious mind, the part of your mind that retains memories and feelings and directs your beliefs and behaviour.

  When hardwired beliefs are installed during the early years of life, the brain behaves like a sponge and operates at the theta frequency. Additionally, the minds of people who report deep spiritual connections are typically operating in this range of frequencies. This is where more instantaneous change can take place.

- **Delta waves** have a frequency of 0–4 Hz. They occur when you're in a deep, dreamless sleep. This state is most often found in young children and is involved in our unconscious bodily functions. Some people who are able to do deep, transcendental meditation also get into delta. In this frequency, you feel totally detached. A lot of healing occurs in this state, which is why quality sleep is so important.

Your default operating system, centred around your head brain, vibrates at a fast beta frequency. The Connection Practice will teach you to drop down into a slower frequency such as alpha and allow your brain to function at an optimum level where it can access insights and grow new neural connections using bursts of gamma.

Changing our state of mind is a valuable skill, as it allows us to navigate through life in the best way for our health and the way that achieves the best results. In addition, there is another reason that changing mind states is valuable, and this is linked to the use of our mirror neurons.

Mirror neurons

Did you know that you can change the emotional state of other people within two minutes?

How do you do this?

Neuroscience has shown that the brain has *mirror neurons* that enable you to pick up subtle emotional cues and feelings of others without being consciously aware that you are doing so. Information from the mirror neurons is processed very quickly. If you are the first to manage your emotional state in an interaction, you set the tone or climate in the room or conversation and can shift the emotional state of others. That's how powerful this is. Our emotions are literally contagious!

Have you ever been with a group of people when one person started to laugh, and you couldn't help but laugh too? Try walking down the street and smiling at people you pass, and notice the effect that it has.

Once you pick up on the feelings of the others, if you are aware enough you can choose how to behave in response. The feedback from mirror neurons is a two-way process. The impact of this is that we are constantly influencing each other's mood, judgments and behaviours. This ability creates resonance with others. In other words, it enables us to be on the same wavelength.

When we (Sue and Penny) first met, there was an instant connection, and often when we facilitate workshops, people comment on how seamlessly we work together. Have you ever experienced that immediate chemistry with anyone?

Neuroscience shows that there are several ways in which you can intentionally influence your state of mind. These include:

- Changing your brain chemically
- Rewiring your brain
- Altering the frequency your brain is operating in
- Through the use of mirror neurons

Quantum science

The second doctrine of New Science is *quantum science*, which describes the behaviour of the smallest particles of energy that make up the universe. This takes us further in understanding our relationships with our environment. There are three key relevant principles we will explore:

1. Everything is made of energy
2. All energy is interconnected; therefore, everything is interconnected
3. The energy of something is brought into reality when it is focused on

The first principle of quantum science is that everything is made of energy. Nobel Prize-winning physicists have proven that the physical world is a matrix of energy. There are two types of energy. From a traditional physics perspective, there is the kind of energy that can be measured in quantifiable units. In addition to this, there is also *subtle energy*. This is a more subjective kind of energy that individuals sense and feel; yet it can create tangible and physical sensations. Subtle energy is gradually starting to be more understood in quantum science.

However, ancient Eastern cultures have understood these energy systems for thousands of years – for example, how the *chi/qi*, the universal life energy of our body, connects to the energy around us. Also, in some Indian cultures a *chakra* is thought to be an energy centre in the body. Chakras are believed to be part of the subtle body, which overlays the physical body and, as such, are the meeting points of the subtle (nonphysical) energy channel, through which the life-force *prana* or vital energy (nonphysical) moves and flows.

In these traditions, there are seven basic chakras, and through modern physiology we can see that these seven chakras correspond exactly to the seven main nerve clusters, which emanate from the spinal column to the organs and specific regions of the body. It is believed that blocked energy in any one of the seven chakras can lead to illness in the corresponding body parts, so it's important to keep this energy flowing freely.

Some religions talk about the *soul* or *spirit*, referring to an awareness of a particular type of subtle energy. Also, the concept of 'oneness' in some spiritual teachings and everything being connected, all now have a scientific basis.

Our connection with the energy world is often referred to as our level of consciousness or awareness, something that is not easy to describe in words; it is something we have to directly experience.

The second principle of quantum science is that all energy is interconnected; therefore, everything is interconnected. Put in simple terms, everything is made of energy and all of that energy is interconnected. The space around us is actually filled with tiny vibrating particles. This aliveness is the life-force energy that connects all things. All people and objects share this connecting energy field.

So, there are two ways of looking at reality. The external reality where everything appears solid and separate, or a deeper reality where everything is made of interconnecting energy. For example, things that are solid, fluid or gas are all made of energy; they are just vibrating at different frequencies.

Your body appears to be a solid physical structure; however, in reality it is an ever-flowing river of information and energy in constant dynamic exchange with the environment around you. Your physical body, your thoughts, emotions and the universe are all composed of the same energy. The universe and all it contains come from the same source. If you become consciously aware of this, you can sense that you are actually connected to everyone and everything.

When you are able to sense people, you're not only able to use your mirror neurons, but you're also intuitively aware at an ener-getic level. You might say:

- His words really resonated with me
- I got a bad vibe from that person
- My friend has such a good heart

These are not just metaphors; we really do feel each other's energy and are affected by it subtly and at a profound level. Think of all the qualities that you intuitively sense on an energetic level in another person. Besides telling if someone is happy or sad, you can tell if they are peaceful or burdened. Looking into their eyes reveals openness or dullness or tenderness or indifference – all human qualities have an energy signature.

Your thoughts are energy and change the universe on a particle-by-particle basis to create a physical life. You affect everything in your world through the energy you put out. Like energy attracts like energy. Your energy is your greatest source of power – the energy you put out is what you will receive; when you send out a high vibration, you receive a high vibration back. So be careful what you think!

How can you become aware of or connect into this energy field? As the diagram shows, once your three brains are fully connected, you can access your whole self or your fully connected brain. This access enables you not only to take in impulses from the three brains, but also to take in the impulses and signals from the wider energy field around you. This allows you to shift to a *quantum level of intelligence* (also known as QQ) where you are connected and able to tune into your innate abilities, such as your intuition, knowing and sensing. You can then access your wisdom, genius, heightened creativity and full potential.

The three brains and the full-connection brain

—

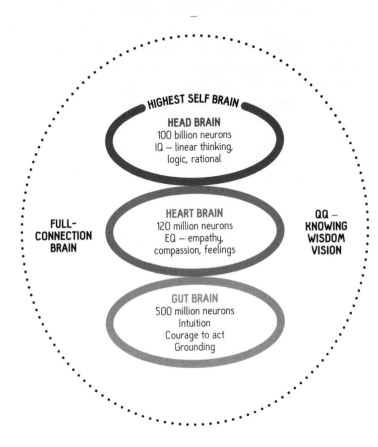

The third principle of quantum science is that observation energizes the subject of your attention. When we engage with something or someone, we focus our energy there and by doing so, bring it into reality. Energy flows where your attention goes. This refers to our ability to create and manifest. We are the masters of our lives and have the ability to choose and create the life we want. We will give you the key secrets to manifesting in Chapter 8, Creating an Abundant Life.

OUR EMOTIONS ARE ENERGY AND HAVE FREQUENCIES TOO

Earlier in the chapter we explored brainwave frequencies. In this section on quantum science we have said that everything is energy, and that this includes our thoughts and emotions.

Our thoughts are energy impulses. Every thought we have triggers an emotional response. Our emotions determine the *vibrational frequency* that we put out into the world. Consequently, whatever you are thinking not only influences the vibration of your energy field, but the vibration of the world around you. These vibrations can have a lasting impact.

One iconic example is the Taj Mahal, which is widely considered to be one of the most beautiful buildings ever created. This exquisite marble structure in Agra, India, is a monument to the love of a husband for his favourite wife. When you visit this wonderful place, the vibration of the love with which the building was created is palpable.

Love-based thoughts feel light and positive and have a high vibrational frequency. Love energy feels positive because it connects people. In contrast, fear-based thoughts feel heavy and negative and have a low vibrational frequency. Fear-energy feels negative because it separates people. It goes against the natural energetic order of things.

Emotional frequencies

In his book *Power vs Force*, David R. Hawkins classifies the principal human emotions according to their frequency of vibration. We have expanded this here by adding in complimentary information from other sources.

The range of emotional frequencies

—

Frequency Hz	Level	Feeling
700–1,000	Illumination/oneness	Enlightenment
700–900	Gratitude	Appreciation
600	Peace/harmony	Bliss
540	Unconditional love	Serenity
528–741	Abundance	Fulfilment
528	Love	Reverence
432	Happiness	Contentment
350	Acceptance	Forgiveness
250	Neutrality/quiet centre of stillness/present in the moment	Trust
200–400	Courage	Affirmation
175	Pride/vanity/envy/jealousy/judgment	Scorn
150	Anger	Hate
125	Desire	Craving
100	Fear/abandonment/worry/shock	Anxiety/stress
75	Grief/sorrow/sadness/loneliness/rejection	Regret
50	Apathy	Despair/depression
30	Guilt	Blame/remorse
20	Shame	Humiliation

At the bottom of the vibrational scale is **shame** (20 Hz) and **guilt** (30 Hz) based on self-hatred. Shame is related to humiliation, low self-esteem and paranoia. Guilt brings feelings of remorse.

Next comes **apathy** (50 Hz). This is about hopelessness, despair and depression. People here are needy and people tend to avoid them.

This is followed by **grief** (75 Hz). Based on loss and regret, it brings great sadness. It is based in the past.

Fear is the next level (100 Hz), which, while it is negative, has more energy and can energize us to move away from what we don't want. Fear is usually experienced as worry, anxiety or panic.

All of the negative emotions tend to reinforce each other and often occur together. They are based on a belief that happiness is something to be found on the outside of oneself, which leads to powerlessness and weakness. There is a mindset of separation rather than connection. According to Hawkins, about one third of the world's population live with low vibrational frequency associated with the states of fear, grief and apathy. Some 85% are at a frequency of 200 Hz or below.

Desire (125 Hz) is still in the negative energy field. This is about craving, obsession and compulsion. It can fuel people to be successful and make a lot of money.

Anger comes next (150 Hz). This is a high-energy emotion and if used constructively can fuel determination and help to move us up to the next level of emotion. On the other hand, it can be destructive and lead to hatred, grudges, and even murder or war. People at this energetic level can be experienced as toxic people.

Pride (175 Hz) leads to a closed mind; the need to be right and a fear of being wrong can lead to denial. Nothing is good enough.

As we move up the scale, the first level of being in our true power, where we stop sleepwalking through life, is **courage**

(200–400 Hz). At this level, we value truth and integrity rather than falsehood and short-term gain. Courage brings empowerment.

Trust is the next level up at 250 Hz. This is about self-trust. It is about being neutral and letting go of either resistance or attachment and not being judgmental.

Acceptance (350 Hz) is about being capable and confident. Transformation starts to happen here as we realize that we are the source of our own happiness and that the power is within us. It is about reclaiming your own power.

Happiness (432 Hz) is an inner attitude of positive enthusiasm, which makes you attractive to others, makes you want to share your happiness with others, and generates the sort of success that breeds deep satisfaction in your life.

Love (528 Hz) leads to a paradigm shift in consciousness. Love is of the heart. It is an expression of our inner happiness.

Abundance (528–741 Hz) is plentifulness of the good things in life. Abundance is a state of mind. It is about what brings you joy and fulfilment, not about what you have.

Unconditional love (540 Hz) is the energy of healing. We feel inner serenity and compassion and yet feel more alive and full of joy. We appreciate the beauty of the world and see life through a positive lens. We have a sense of connection and unity.

Peace (600 Hz) leads to a feeling of bliss. Everything is perceived as interconnected. There is no longer any distinction between the observer and the subject. Hawkins claims that this level is only attained by one out of ten million people.

Gratitude (700–900 Hz) raises your vibrational frequency because it makes you aware of all the things you love and how abundant your life really is. Expressing gratitude for any situation projects a magnetic force that draws to you more of what you are expressing gratitude for.

Oneness (700–1,000 Hz) is a sense of being one with everything in the universe. This is explained by quantum science as a unified field, which underlies and connects everything in creation.

Prolonged periods of time spent at the lower levels (20–175 Hz) of the vibrational scale lead to sickness and disease in the body and feelings of despair and hopelessness in the mind.

Prolonged periods of time spent at the upper end of the vibrational scale (250–1,000 Hz), above the level of trust, lead to health in the body and feelings of joy and wellbeing in the mind. When we are happy, we experience energetic coherence, connection and flow.

THE JOURNEY TO CONNECTION: BEING AWARE AND CONSCIOUS

By exploring and understanding your psychological and scientific operating systems, you can open up to a whole host of information that will provide awareness of what amazing beings we all are. You see how it is possible to get tripped up and the opportunities that are available to us.

As discussed earlier, most of the time your brain uses the default operating system to take in the huge volume of information received from the outside world; it then filters it through your memories and interprets it. This process tends to be past-referenced thought and often fear-based. This causes a physical and emotional reaction in your body, causing you to close down and unconsciously react as in the response to stress. In this case, as we mentioned earlier, your thinking brain shuts down and you have impaired functioning.

Default stress-creating operating system

—

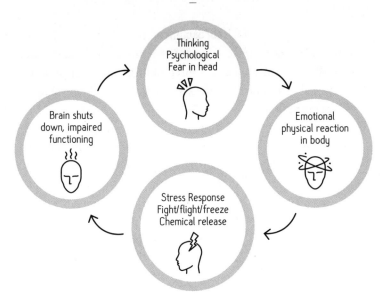

How do you switch from that default operating system to one where you consciously choose how to respond? We share this with you in Chapter 4, Opening Up.

Imagine what it would be like to easily manage your energetic state so that you are able to shift from your default operating system to a state of full connection as and when you choose. How to access this full-connection operating system is the secret that we will share with you in the next chapter. The opportunity from there is to access the ZOC, get into flow, and be fully present and tuned into what is happening in the moment.

In short
KEY CONCEPTS THAT UNDERPIN THE ZOC

Neuroscience

- It has been shown that we have three brains; head, heart and gut. When connected to all three brains, you enter an autonomic balance and coherence, an optimal state of neurological balance and flow
- The brain has an overarching organizing principle that classifies the world into things that either hurt you or help you to stay alive, resulting in either the away or toward state
- Due to its neuroplasticity, our brain is amazingly adaptable, its capacity to continue to grow and rewire itself enables us to learn and change continuously
- Through your mirror neurons you can set the tone and change the emotional state of other people within two minutes – our emotions are literally contagious!

Quantum science

- Quantum science has three key principles: everything is made of energy, all energy is interconnected; therefore, everything is interconnected, and the energy of something is brought into reality when it is focussed on
- We create our reality through our thoughts and where we focus our attention; in the material world we transform 'thought energy' into matter
- All human qualities have an energy signature – your energy is your greatest source of power
- Our emotions are energy and have frequencies – our emotions determine the vibrational frequency that we put out into the world

Psychology

- The energetic self grows and develops in stages; your psychological and energetic development follow parallel journeys
- Our growth and development can be hindered by limiting beliefs, automatic patterns, and blocked emotions
- The Connection Practice goes beyond mindfulness and offers an alternative to our default autopilot operating system and stress response
- The Connection Practice will enable you to shift from your default operating system to a state of full connection (ZOC) as and when you choose

Your Reflections

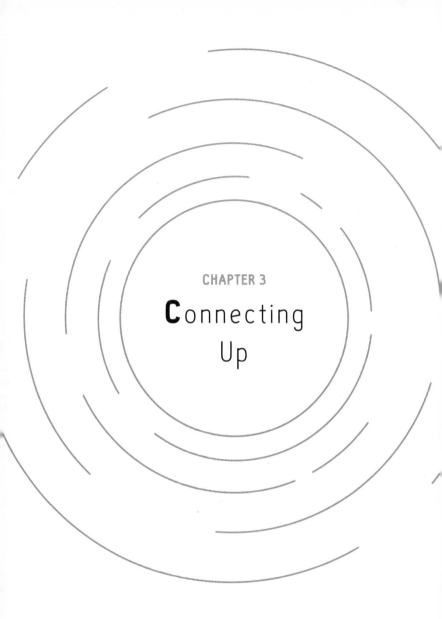

CHAPTER 3

Connecting Up

"Most of us walk around as if we're sleepwalking. We really
don't experience the world fully, because we're half-asleep,
doing things we automatically think we have to do."
Mitch Albom

Back in 2004, we were sick of feeling stuck and unhappy, doing things automatically, and repeating the same old negative thought and behaviour patterns. Gradually we realized that what had got us to that negative mindset would keep us stuck there and we would only be able to shift into a new place if we found a way to change our energetic state.

By changing your state of being, your experience will follow. By shifting the energy, changing the vibrational frequency or vibe, you will find that you can be in a new place. The key to making this profound shift is learning to manage your energetic state, which is what the Connection Practice did for us and will do for you.

THE CONNECTION PRACTICE

What is the Connection Practice? It is a practice that we developed to enable us to switch from being on autopilot to a new, fully connected operating system and one that would enable us to reboot ourselves whenever we want to. Waking up and getting into the ZOC is one of the secrets to living a wonderful life of your choice.

Perhaps you find that at times during the day there are negative or repetitive thoughts in your head, thoughts that bring up stressful feelings that affect you adversely. Possibly you allow yourself to continually get distracted and feel exhausted by the end of the day. You'll recognize the signs: speeding up, cramming too much in, suffering headaches or pain in your body, irritability and anxiety, going to bed late, not getting enough sleep, procrastinating, and zoning out with mindless TV and screen addiction.

You may feel a lack of laughter and joy, droning on through the weekdays, looking forward to weekends and feeling as though life is a never-ending rat race. Complaining that things are not as they could be.

Maybe you find yourself being affected and pressured by other people and events, and you're not able to stay centred and balanced; instead you are reactive and unconscious of the choices available to you. Perhaps you have started to recognize that you would like to create change and have a choice.

So, what would you change?

Maybe you would like to wake up each day feeling positive, looking forward to the day ahead. Sense what it would be like to feel really good about yourself and to treat yourself with kindness, to feel connected to yourself, others and life. To have that feeling of enjoying every moment, so that you feel energized by the joy of being alive and living life to the fullest. Here you are in the zone, your life is flowing naturally, you have a sense of wellbeing and feel happy. You see things from a fresh perspective, you are open, curious and ready to grow, and you see a world that is full of possibilities. A world in which you are able to manage difficulties with ease, develop new ways of responding and are empowered to choose.

Ask yourself: how effective are my current strategies for creating the life I want?

In this chapter, we will look at how the Connection Practice can support you in moving from disconnection and living on autopilot to the full-connection operating system. We explain in detail what it is and how the Connection Practice works, but then more importantly we provide you with guidance so that you have the opportunity to directly experience it. Training yourself in this new way of being through regular practice will mean that you can change your state in the moment as easily as flicking a switch. We call this Instant Connection.

The essence of this easy and quick routine is to create a core connection that lets you feel grounded, open, present with all of who you are, and expanded in flow or in the zone – and to be so whenever you choose to be.

You will start to avoid getting caught on autopilot, feeling disconnected, and unconsciously repeating unhelpful patterns and habits. As you start to learn a new way of being connected in your life, you will become more aware and have the opportunity to interrupt those patterns and make effective choices.

The Connection Practice short-circuits your subconscious mind and past conditioning, creating new positive pathways so that you can create the life you want. It enables you to orchestrate the different pieces of your life to flow together, creating the life you desire.

To put this into context now, let's explore the different levels of connection.

THREE LEVELS OF CONNECTION

From our experience and through distilling the many theories that we have studied, we believe that there are three levels for engaging and connecting with life.

Level 1: disconnection – being unaware

This is when we are stuck with only our head brain engaged, with a beta brainwave and low emotional frequency from 75–150 Hz. This is the vibrational energy of grief, fear, desire and anger (see the 'Range of emotional frequencies' table on page 43). We are confined to a mental intelligence (IQ) based on only using logic and linear thinking. We are distracted, unaware and fused with the unconscious thoughts that drive our behaviour. We see ourselves as separate, operating more in ego/personality and from our small self, and can feel stressed and anxious with our story/drama becoming all-consuming. We very often focus on the past, future projections, comparisons, judgments, and feelings associated with being separate.

This is a state of *No Presence*. We're operating from a tiny, limited perspective based on habitual patterns and behaviours, consumed by our thoughts, only realizing a fragment of our potential. This is what it is like when we are in our default operating system with our ego mind dominating and preventing us from expanding and evolving.

As we start to move, step by step, from being disconnected, we bring more of the suppressed beliefs, emotions and patterns that are keeping us stuck and disconnected into conscious awareness, where we can be ready to let go of them.

Level 2: mindful connection – being aware

This is the first step toward starting to choose how we respond as opposed to allowing our head brain and conditioning to react automatically.

At this level of connection, we use the mind and the body. The three brains connect to create the mind-body. This uses all of our senses and connects the neurons and nerve endings in the head, heart and gut brains. It accesses our alpha brainwave frequency and produces positive chemicals to support our sense of wellbeing.

We feel centred and grounded, fully present in the here and now. Present awareness is the key to mindfulness. This is a state of nonjudgmental, nonreactive awareness – a more natural, still and relaxed state. In this state, when we are open and relaxed, we experience more of life's pleasure, which is what we are after! Whereas, when we are not present, we are tense and resist, and we feel pain.

We can observe the processes of the mind and body, becoming aware of our unconscious, automatic propensities – our habits, behaviours and feelings. With this awareness, we have the chance to step out of our automatic programming.

In this state, we are defused from our thoughts, connected to our body, and aware of what is happening in us, around us and in others. We are likely to be more emotionally intelligent (EQ) and can manage our emotions better and also pick up on the emotions of others. We can choose how we respond and see things more objectively.

We are connected to our true nature and begin to see things from a place of present awareness. We are open to present experiences that arise, trusting our ability to deal with them in the moment. Our vibrational frequency is raised to between 250 and 350 Hz.

Level 3: full connection – expanded, in the ZOC and in your true power

At this advanced level of connection, we have expanded awareness and are in a conscious state. When we are connected to our mind, body *and* whole being, we are in the full-connection operating system – this is where you go beyond mindfulness and begin to experience 'zone-fulness'! Your vibrational frequency is up between 500 and 1,000 Hz.

This can be achieved by shifting from the left-brain dominance to the right-brain connection. In doing so, our head, heart and gut brains start to operate together to access a higher quantum level of intelligence.

This quantum level of intelligence is where wisdom emerges, and we have clarity, insight and inspiration.

We access our full self, a state in which the confines of mind and body, of our minute inner world, disappear, and we shift to accessing a more natural state in which we are fully present and connected to our whole, vibrant being and the vast outer world.

We are aware of and open to a deeper reality, where everything is made of energy, including us, and we experience the interconnectedness of all things and have a wider, more expanded perspective.

As you operate from full connection, and by being 'in the ZOC', you are able to access wisdom, creativity, vision, passion and purpose, peace, happiness, love, joy, genius and brilliance. When you enter this state, all realizations and possibilities exist. Ultimately, you sense the energy of your full potential, unconstrained by your conditioned thought. You tap into a much larger, more visionary energy and are able to see through the details to connect to the bigger purpose.

You are the creator of your own life and have a far-reaching transformational impact on yourself and the world around you.

One of our actress clients found that the Connection Practice allowed her "to connect to a bigger sense of self. I walk taller and have a greater sense of my own unlimited expansion. I have used this expansion countless times. It helps with personal power and maintaining a sense of self in many situations. It has transformed not only my presence as an actress, but also my relationships."

HOW DO WE GET INTO FULL CONNECTION?

By this stage in the book, you have engaged your neocortex, the intellectual, philosophical, rational, thinking part of your brain. Now what we are looking to do is apply the information with the intention of changing your actions and behaviours. This requires your mind and body to work together to create the experience of how it feels when you practise the Connection Practice and enter a state of full connection.

We know that we only change our experience when we change our actions. Let's go for it!

In order for you to experience the exercises in the remainder of this chapter you have the following options:

1. The best way is to download the audio versions of the exercises by following the link below or scanning the assigned QR code:
   thezoneofconnection.com/downloads
2. You can read aloud and record the exercises on your phone and then experience them as you play them back
3. You can practise them by following the step-by-step guide in the book

Exercise 1

Step-by-step explanation and experience of the Connection Practice

In order to clearly see what the Connection Practice can do for you, we have broken it down into five simple steps. For each step we demonstrate why it matters, what it entails and what effect it will have, and have written a practice for you to follow and experience.

The aim of the Connection Practice is to take you from mind to body to an expanded and fully connected state of being 'in the ZOC', where you can access your whole being. You now know that you have all the biological and neurological machinery to do this and do it naturally.

Of the five steps to full connection, the first three (A, B and C) take you to mindful connection. Steps D and E than take you to full connection:

Step A: Aim and setting intentions

Step B: Balance and posture

Step C: Conscious breathing

Step D: Deepening through alignment and grounding

Step E: Expansion to full connection

Once you are familiar with the Connection Practice and your mind and body get used to knowing and experiencing this, you can start to use Fast Connection, then Instant Connection, which are practices that we have developed to provide you with quick access to full connection.

As you continue to practise, you will eventually be able to get to full-connection living and zone-fulness in just a few minutes. Our intention is to inspire you to apply, practise and integrate this to enrich your daily life.

As you try out each step, we suggest that you find a place where you will not be disturbed. Be open-minded, playful and willing to experiment. Do it in a way that works for you. If you can, it's best to start doing it standing up, but if you're uncomfortable please feel free to do it sitting down. Definitely don't attempt any of this while driving, as you will most likely want to close your eyes, at least to begin with!

STEP A: AIM AND SETTING INTENTIONS

Why does setting intentions matter?

Quantum science shows us that what we focus our intention and energy on becomes the reality we experience. The context we set when we put out an intention shapes all that follows, ultimately determining the outcome of the situation.

Focusing the mind on your aim or intention starts the process of rewiring your brain, giving you the opportunity to break patterns and habits that don't work for you, consciously setting the path that does.

What does it entail?

First, you go inside and tune into what the best outcome or possibility would be. Then you imagine and visualize that happening and align yourself with it.

What impact will this have on me?

This exerts an energetic focus and a positive influence on your thoughts and actions.

Without intention, your actions are unguided, but without action your intentions get you nowhere. In order to maximize your effectiveness in achieving what you want to accomplish, you need to have maximum intention, like a guiding light pulling you toward the outcome.

The power of setting intentions is huge. Through the power of your intentions, you can reorganize your energy in an instant, because your intentions create your reality. An example is how athletes, before performing, visualize the race and desired outcome, setting themselves up so that their mind and body are aligned behind their aim, driving them toward it regardless of their chances of success.

It's good practice to always start your day by setting intentions, so that what you want to happen comes about.

Let's practise setting intentions

○ Close your eyes and set your intention to experience a state of full
   connection. Take a moment to imagine that possibility for yourself
   and say YES to it

STEP B: BALANCE

Why does creating balance matter?

This is the first stage of a mindful connection. When we are tense and
closed, we are stuck in our repetitive and sometimes negative thoughts.
To shift away from this, we need to get our mind and body into a more
open and relaxed state. The habit of feeling open and relaxed is part of
rewiring our brain to create what is called a toward state. This gives you a
sense of inner balance and allows your body to come into a more natural
and relaxed state supported by good posture. Using quantum awareness
to sense the invisible energy around you, you feel for balance within that
atmosphere, allowing you to relax more, let go and feel supported.

What does it entail?

You start to slow down on the inside and use your mind to observe how
you are feeling. You let go of any tension in your body, as this is the key
to experiencing more of yourself.

What effect will it have?

Being aware of when our posture is aligned and balanced helps our body
to function at its best, and you feel more confident in any situation as
your posture improves.

This key step starts the process of experiencing more of yourself by
taking your attention out of your continual stream of thoughts and into
your body.

It's exhausting being consumed by thoughts, and this is the root of all
stress and anxiety. As you connect with your body, you become aware
of how tense or relaxed you are. You become aware that you have
energetic sensations in your body and around your body.

Feeling connected to gravity and the energy force around you will help to soften and relax in your core. In this natural, relaxed state, you will feel more present, peaceful and calm. Trusting that you are safe and supported brings you back from any fear or anxiety you may have been feeling.

Let's practise creating balance now

○ Lengthen your spine and open your chest, feel a posture of uprightness and openness, feeling supported with a sense of integrity and alignment.

○ Relax your jaw and shoulders — let gravity have them

○ Soften your heart and relax your pelvic floor

○ Start to allow yourself to become aware of what's going on right now in this moment

○ Take a moment to observe what is going on in your thoughts, your feelings and your body, notice any sensations with a sense of acceptance

Extending beyond your physical body is your energy body, which is a sphere that surrounds you. We are now going to feel for balance within your energy body.

○ Allow yourself to wonder and explore what it would be like if your energy was equal and even at the back and front of your body. If it helps, you can imagine your energy field as a colour or texture. To the right and left of your body. Above your head and below your body. Take a moment to feel for that balance. Allow yourself to rest in the safety of your field and trust it to support you

STEP C: CONSCIOUS BREATHING

Why does conscious breathing and letting go matter?

This is the second stage of mindful connection. Breath is important in this stage because the quality and tone of your breathing directly influences your state, as it can slow and calm you down. Conscious breathing redefines your awareness. Presence or in-the-moment awareness is important as it short-circuits your subconscious and past conditioning, creating new pathways for living.

Your breath connects your mind and your body and in so doing connects your head brain to your heart and gut brain, bringing you to autonomic balance and a state of mindful connection.

Past emotions can get stuck in the body and cause tension; the breath is a useful tool to dissipate this tension and let it go.

What does it entail?

You use the breath to deepen your awareness of what is going on in your body. As you notice tension, you can use the breath to release it.

You recognize that the body automatically breathes on its own, and you can allow the body to breathe when it is ready. This helps you to relax and let go of your need to control.

Through conscious breathing you connect mind and body, slow down and come into a state of mindful connection.

What effect will it have on me?

The simple act of being aware of your breath is an important part of your self-support system. By using the breath to connect into the belly, you will connect with your gut feelings, through your knowing (see innate abilities in Chapter 5) you have greater awareness and a deep confidence. Being present turns up the volume in your life.

Being connected to each breath will slow you down. It is like an anchor that continually brings you back into the present moment. This gives you the opportunity to take a breathing space in which you can step out of autopilot.

We all go in and out of being present, but with practice we start to develop an awareness of the things that cause us to lose it. We learn to use our breath to expel from our body and let go of the things that stop us from being present in the moment, and then we are able to use the breath to bring us back into mindful connection.

In mindful connection, you experience the stillness behind your breath, and the sense of stillness inside means you are more in touch with who you really are. With the breath, you are tuned into awareness, the part of you that is experiencing this moment, instead of the jumble of thoughts in your head. You begin to understand that you are not your thoughts; you are much bigger, deeper and wider than your thoughts.

You are in a relaxed, natural state from which you can observe the processes of your mind and body, step out of your programming, become more conscious of your unconscious patterns and become less reactive. In this place, you are aware that you can change these unhelpful patterns and are ready to do the inner work to bring this about. This is particularly useful for interrupting reactions such as the stress response or anxiety, to self-regulate and get yourself back into a stable state. Here you are in touch with your emotional intelligence (EQ), with a better mechanism for managing your emotions and have the capacity to show empathy for others.

Let's practise letting go now

○ Take a moment to become aware of your breath and notice where it is in your body

○ Now start by taking some big breaths in through your nose then sighing it out through your mouth. With each breath let go of anything that you don't need, anything that is stopping you from being present right here and now. Keep letting go and you will gradually come back to who you really are. Do this cleansing breathing exercise a few times

Let's practise conscious breathing now

○ Now you are going to inhale for a count of six, pause until your body naturally wants to breathe out and exhale for a count of six. As you breathe in slowly and fully through your nose, allow your belly to swell and expand. The belly is the seat of your sense of presence, knowing and deep confidence. Breathe your energy down from your head into your heart and gut brain to connect your entire body

○ Pause, and repeat this two more times

○ Feel yourself calming down and a sense of stillness

○ As you enjoy this state of mindful connection, notice how you feel, notice your beautiful inner smile and notice how present you are now

STEP D: DEEPENING THROUGH ALIGNMENT AND GROUNDING

Why does being centred, aligned and grounded matter?

In martial arts, it's said that centredness must come from the *hara* (the belly), which takes its initial strength from the alignment of the head, shoulders, hips, knees and feet. We must be aligned for the energy chakras to be balanced and to allow our energy to flow between them.

Feeling grounded with the earth under our feet gives us a sense of stability and a strong base from which to respond in the moment making good choices.

What does it entail?

The process allows you to have a sense of being centred, grounded and aligned. This deepens the balance within the body, giving you a strong base from which to start the expansion of your awareness beyond the body.

You learn to align yourself between the light, radiant energy of the sun and the source energy of the earth.

What effect will it have?

As you follow the exercise, you will get a sense of connecting your inner energy channel and centres, possibly feeling the different energy hubs in your body, opening you up from the inside out. This is the beginning of connecting beyond your body.

Feeling grounded through the earth and yet connected to something bigger, you can feel your own centre in relation to the world around you. This brings you deeper into being present. Centred, grounded and present, you can objectively choose how you respond in your daily challenges.

Let's practise centring, aligning and grounding now

○ With your eyes closed, bring your attention to the centre point of your chest, imagine a line going up through your throat, behind your eyes and out through the crown of your head

- Then imagine this line extending up through the sky, through the atmosphere of the earth and all the way to the centre of the sun. Enjoy the beautiful warmth and feel connected to the radiant light energy of the sun for a moment or two
- Then start to move your attention back down this line, back into your body through the crown of your head. Slowly move down behind your eyes, through your throat, through your heart, solar plexus, and belly, down into your pelvis, out through your tailbone. Keep following the line down your legs and through your feet to the earth and get in touch with its the deep red-hot molten core. Feel grounded with your feet firmly rooted. Take a moment to feel deeply connected to beautiful mother earth and your source energy
- Then when you are ready, move your attention slowly back up the line through the earth, feel the energy tingling around your feet, then back into your body, your legs, and to your belly and feel centred
- As you rest your attention in your centre, keep a sense of the line in place running all the way from the earth through your body and up to the centre of the sun — feeling fully grounded, centred and aligned

STEP E: EXPANSION

Why does expansion matter?

This is the final step to full connection. We understand that everything is made up of energy and that all energy is interconnected. In this step we start to experience this principle for ourselves and recognize that our whole being is actually a field of energy that is connected to the entire energy world. We are able to connect with the intelligence in the wider energy field. It's like connecting your computer up to the internet; all of that wider intelligence is available to download. When all of our intelligences operate together in this way, generative wisdom emerges through quantum intelligence.

We see that our energy expands outside of us, and is connected to and has a direct impact on everything around us — feeling connected to it with no separation. In this fully connected state, we access flow and are in the ZOC.

What impact does full connection have on the brain?

In this expanded state, there is a positive effect on the chemistry in the body. Our brain generates more of the 'happy chemicals' and less of the damaging, stress-related chemicals. Changing our body's chemistry and neurology conditions our brain and body for optimum functioning and gives us a sense of health and wellbeing. Being expanded regularly creates new pathways that break and replace negative habits and patterns, generating a positive effect on our lives.

This is the full-connection operating system. You are now flowing in the ZOC and beginning to be in your true power.

What does it entail?

It's important to feel grounded and present before you expand your energy outside of your body.

First, you must sense your energy inside of your body, how it feels and what you are experiencing. Then, extending your awareness and energy beyond the confines of your body, you can notice how it feels to be fully connected in this way. You realize that you are not just a body but also a field of energy that affects everything.

What effect will it have on me?

You have a wider, more expanded experience shifting to access a more natural state where you are fully present, and connected to your whole full, vibrant self and everything in the vast, outer world. Waves of energy flow from inside to outside as your field of presence emanates out around you, and you have an expanded focus.

When you are in this state of being, you access flow, the zone of peak performance.

Like an athlete, you are totally in the moment, time seems to slow, and you feel relaxed, fully and magnificently alive, present and alert with heightened senses. With your energy flowing, you have a sense that everything is just right, you are exhilarated by life, inspired and inspiring, fully conscious, aware, connected and expanded to everything and everyone.

Living from full connection, you have the possibility of creating the life you desire and have a transformative effect on the world around you.

Let's practise expansion

- With your eyes closed, start to imagine a ball of energy in your heart centre in your chest. It may have colour, movement, texture, shape – just allow yourself to sense, feel or visualize this ball of energy. Really get a sense of your heart opening as this ball of energy starts to expand so that it fills your whole chest area

- Now imagine letting this ball of energy get bigger, and as it expands imagine that it starts to fill your entire body

- Then allow it to get even bigger so that it expands outward beyond your body and starts to merge with the energy that is outside of your body, all around you

- Your feet stay anchored on the ground and the ball of energy keeps getting bigger – filling the room that you are in, then the building, then beyond that to the biggest, vastest it can be, way out there, even bigger than the earth, past the planets, to include the whole universe. Expand out until you connect to the vibrant light energy, connecting to the oneness and source energy that holds everything together. Allow yourself to experience this larger dimension

- When you go out to that space you can keep connecting and connecting. You don't have an edge or an end to you, you can keep going and going. This is because you are an infinite being in a body, who can perceive and know anything and in this space you can reprogram anything

- Feel yourself centred, anchored by your presence right here in this moment. Feel your connection to that massive outer world of vibrant interconnected energy

- Simply notice and observe how this feels and how big your expanded energy field now is

- Feel the sense of peacefulness that resonates inside your body

- Gently open your eyes and start to feel your presence and energy expanded into the space around you

- Take a few steps around the room in this expanded state. Notice how your energy is connected to all things in the room and how it affects the space, the room and the world around you
- Walking vibrantly in the world, as you feel connected to everything you send the message that we are all in this together
- This state will let you live from this deeper place so that you feel more connected to the delight of being all that nature has. Realizing that we are not just a body, but also a field of energy that has a direct effect on the world around us. You can develop your own life-force in flow of the bigger transformative energy field
- How do you feel now? You might want to make a note in your journal of your experience

Now we are ready to experience the full version of the Connection Practice with all of the five steps listed below linked up:
- **Step A:** Aim – intention
- **Step B:** Balance – posture
- **Step C:** Conscious Breathing – letting go
- **Step D:** Deepening through centring, alignment and grounding
- **Step E:** Expansion to full connection

The following exercise is about shifting from our heads or personality/ego state to allowing our body to feel grounded, then expanding to our whole being where we can feel more present, in flow and consciously aware. With practice, this process enables access to the state of full connection.

Exercise 2
The Full Connection Practice

Again, find a place where you will not be disturbed.

Create a safe space, where you are noticing, not judging – just being yourself. There is no right or wrong experience; whatever you feel is just right for you. Have an open mind and be playful and willing to experiment, have fun and let go of past learning.

Your full participation will help you get the most out of it. Do it in a way that works for you, so if we ask you to stand up and you are uncomfortable, please feel free to sit down.

There may be some language you haven't heard before – just trust the process, trust yourself and trust us! It will have a transformational effect on your life and others too.

Before we start, ask yourself, on a scale of 1 to 10 where 10 is the best score, where you are in terms of being fully present in this moment?

Aim – setting intentions

○ Close your eyes now and set your intention to experience a state of full connection. Imagine that possibility for yourself and say YES to it.

Balance and posture

It's best if you stand up for the following exercises and close your eyes.

Posture is important, as our bodies function best when they are in alignment whether we are standing, sitting, or lying down.

○ Lengthen your spine and open your chest, feel a posture of uprightness and openness, feeling supported with a sense of integrity and alignment

○ Reax your jaw and shoulders – let gravity have them

○ Soften your heart and relax your pelvic floor

○ Start to allow yourself to become aware of what's going on right now in this moment

○ Take a moment to observe what is going on in your thoughts, your feelings and your body, notice any sensations with a sense of acceptance

- Extending beyond your physical body is your energy body, which is a sphere that surrounds you. We are now going to feel for balance within your energy body
- Allow yourself to wonder and explore what it would be like if your energy was equal and even at the back and front of your body. If it helps, you can imagine your energy field as a colour or texture. To the right and left of your body. Above your head and below your body. Take a moment to feel for that balance. Allow yourself to rest in the safety of your field and trust it to support you

Conscious breathing – accessing mindful connection

- Take a moment to become aware of your breath and notice where it is in your body
- Now start by taking some big breaths in through your nose then sighing it out through your mouth. With each breath let go of anything that you don't need, anything that is stopping you from being present right here and now. Keep letting go and you will gradually come back to who you really are. Do this cleansing breathing exercise a few times
- Now you are going to inhale for a count of six, pause until your body naturally wants to breathe out and exhale for a count of six. As you breathe in slowly and fully through your nose, allow your belly to swell and expand. The belly is the seat of your sense of presence, knowing and deep confidence. Breathe your energy down from your head into your heart and gut brain to connect your entire body
- Pause, and repeat this two more times
- Feel yourself calming down and a sense of stillness
- As you enjoy this state of mindful connection, notice how you feel, notice your beautiful inner smile and notice how present you are now

Deepening connection – alignment, centring and grounding

- Bring your attention to the centre point of your chest, imagine a line going up through your throat, behind your eyes and out through the crown of your head

○ Then imagine this line extending up through the building that you are in, up through the sky, through the atmosphere of the earth and all the way to the centre of the sun. Enjoy the beautiful warmth and feel connected to the radiant light energy of the sun for a moment or two

○ Then start to move your attention back down this line, back into your body through the crown of your head. Slowly move down behind your eyes, through your throat, through your heart, solar plexus and belly, down into your pelvis and out through your tailbone. Keep following the line down your legs and through your feet to the earth and get in touch with its deep molten core, your source energy. Feel grounded with your feet firmly rooted. Take a moment to feel deeply connected to beautiful mother earth and your source energy

○ Then when you are ready, move your attention slowly back up the line back into your body, your legs, and to your belly and feel centred

○ As you rest your attention in your centre keep a sense of the line in place running all the way from the earth through your body and up to the centre of the sun, feeling fully grounded, centred and aligned

Expansion and connecting – accessing full connection

○ Start to imagine a ball of energy in your heart, centre in your chest. It may have colour, movement, texture, shape – just allow yourself to sense, feel or visualize this ball of energy. Really get a sense of your heart opening as this ball of energy starts to expand so that it fills your whole chest area

○ Now imagine letting this ball of energy get bigger, and as it expands imagine that it starts to fill your entire body

○ Then allow it to get even bigger so that it expands outward beyond your body and starts to merge with the energy that is outside of your body, all around you

○ Your feet stay anchored on the ground and the ball of energy keeps getting bigger – filling the room that you are in, then the building, then beyond that to the biggest, vastest it can be, way out there, even bigger than the earth, past the planets, to include the whole universe. Expand out until you connect to the vibrant light energy, connecting to the oneness and source energy that holds everything together. Allow yourself to experience this larger dimension

- When you go out to that space you can keep connecting and connecting. You don't have an edge or an end to you, you can keep going and going. This is because you are an infinite being in a body, who can perceive and know anything and in this space you can reprogram anything
- Feel yourself centred, anchored by your presence right here in this moment. Feel your connection to that massive outer world of vibrant interconnected energy
- Simply notice and observe how this feels and how big your expanded energy field now is
- Feel the sense of peacefulness that resonates inside your body
- Gently open your eyes and start to feel your presence and energy expanded into the space around you
- Take a few steps around the room in this expanded state. Notice how your energy is connected to all things in the room and how it affects the space, the room and the world around you
- Walking vibrantly in the world, as you feel connected to everything you send the message that we are all in this together
- This state will let you live from this deeper place so that you feel more connected to the delight of being all that nature has. Realizing that we are not just a body, but also a field of energy that has a direct effect on the world around us. You can develop your own lifeforce in flow of the bigger transformative energy field
- How do you feel now? You might want to make a note in your journal of your experience version of the Connection

This is the level of full connection where you are equally connected to yourself, to others and to the energy that is around you.

Developing the ability to access this state of full connection will take practice; you must work with all of yourself until it becomes second nature. It's like a muscle that we can exercise and build, a skill that you are learning. Eventually, you can fully connect almost instantly. When you feel more confident about how you are making this shift, and you are finding it easier to drop into full connection, you can start to try the Fast Connection and work up to Instant Connection (see Exercises 3 and 4). We use Fast Connection in the more advanced exercises later in the book.

Exercise 3
The Fast Connection Practice

- Set your intention to ... (whatever you would like to get out of this practice)
- Feel your feet on the ground and your spine aligned
- Close your eyes
- Notice any sensations in your body and take a moment to allow it to relax
- Bring your attention to the energy surrounding your body and feel for balance in it
- Take a big breath and let go of anything you don't need right here and now
- Breathe in from your head down through your heart to your gut, connecting yourself up
- Take another long conscious, calming breath, slowing down
- From the centre point in your chest start to imagine a line going up through your body and all the way to the centre of the radiant sun
- Now come back down the line into your body and down to the earth all the way to the earth's molten core, your source energy, feeling grounded
- Feel aligned between the sun and the earth
- Sense the energy in your heart centre starting to open and expand into your body
- Allow this energy to expand beyond your body, merging with the energy around you, getting bigger and bigger
- Expand way out into that vibrant energy to encompass the whole earth, out past the planets and connecting to the infinite space of the universe
- As far as you possibly can, imagine where you have no edges and are fully connected to everything
- Notice how you feel now
- Gently open your eyes and feel your energy field in the space around you affecting everything in the world

And when you've really mastered the Fast Connection Practice, you can move to the Instant Connection Practice. As the name suggests, Instant Connection shows you a way to quickly access full connection during your day-to-day activities. It is a way of using the practice in the moment in your daily life when your early warning signs of disconnection first occur or when you want to feel fully connected.

Exercise 4
The Instant Connection Practice

There are three steps to Instant Connection:

Step 1: Focus on your head, notice your thoughts and make a choice to shift your attention

Step 2: Take your awareness down into your body, notice any sensations and allow your body to relax into being centred and grounded, sensing the inner smile in your heart

Step 3: Breathe energy into your body and heart, then as you breathe out, expand your energy and awareness outward, connecting to the vast energy field around you

Eventually you will be able to shorten this even more to be as simple as:

Step 1: HEAD — Breathe energy in through your head and down to your body

Step 2: BODY — Breathe energy out of your body

Step 3: WHOLE — Expand your energy to your whole being

And with lots of practice, one step to full connection!
        EMBODY — WHOLE EXPANDED SELF

FULL CONNECTION LIVING

What do we mean by full connection living?

After the Expansion and Connecting Exercises in Step E of the Connection Practice (Exercises 1 and 2), you will have access to full connection, living where you can:

- Communicate in a way that has a transformational effect on the lives of others
- Set your intentions and bring what you desire into your life
- Have a bigger perspective on life, seeing problems as opportunities, and trusting the flow of life
- Have the opportunity to live in intimate relationship with yourself and others
- See yourself and everyone else as having a greater purpose and potential to make a difference in the world
- Have the ability to use the Law of Attraction to manifest the reality you desire

Living in a full connection state enables you to be all that you can be and to live more consciously and happily. It also enables you to connect to your whole vibrant being, creating the true intimacy that we all crave; we want to experience presence from those we are in relationship with.

Living in this full-connection operating system, we have the possibility of using the energy around us to create the life we desire and have a transformative effect on the world around us.

Use the Connection Practice every day for 21 days so that it starts to become second nature and your brain becomes hard-wired to this operating system. Use the diary date checker at the end of this chapter to support you with this.

The remaining chapters of the book are dedicated to showing you how to use the Connection Practice to:

- Fully experience your authentic self
- Nurture your relationships

- Communicate from full connection
- Manifest and create an abundant life
- Bring about full transformation

What does it entail?

Living in this way, you go beyond being mindful; you reach a state where you are present and fully connected. You can allow your presence (energy field) to expand and connect with the energy around you. You experience the positive qualities of your presence when you are fully connected, as you begin to affect the environment and the people around you. Not only do you feel more alive and connected but so do other people in your presence.

Your energy resonates with those around you and you create more intimate relationships as a result. You take responsibility for the quality of the energy that ripples out from you, knowing that the energy you are sending out will connect with like energy, and that this will all come back to you. In this way, you consciously create your life.

What effect will it have on me?

When we are in full connection, things happen that are often turning points in our lives. Working through the following chapters will give you the opportunity to completely transform your life and have a transformational effect on others. In this book we want to inspire you to make the Connection Practice an integral part of your way of living.

The Connection Practice is a powerful and enjoyable routine that shifts your awareness to a higher vibrational level. Our intention is to provide you with the tools that will support and guide you in practising and using the routine in your daily life. This will result in you being able to access the state of full connection and be in the ZOC at will, whenever and wherever you are. This can easily be integrated into your daily life to support and to enable you to realize the benefits.

Making time to integrate this new practice, and not making the same choices as before, is a powerful way to change your habits. You will only experience the benefits if you practise!

You can teach your body through experience what your mind has intellectually understood. By repeating that experience, you begin to master the routine and it gradually becomes automatic, and you no longer need to think about it. This repetition evolves the circuits in your brain until the routine becomes a habit. You have repeated it so many times that your body knows how to do it, as well as your mind. The routine enables you to innately embody the information, and it becomes who you are.

We encourage you to practise them in the order that they are introduced; Full Connection Practice, then Fast Connection and finally Instant Connection. It's best if you do the Full Connection Practice a few times at least, so you get familiar with the experience of it.

In short
KEY CONCEPTS FOR CONNECTING UP

- When you change your state of being, you can learn to manage your energetic state
- There are three levels of connection: disconnection, mindful connection and full connection
- With regular use of the Connection Practice, you will create new positive pathways and live with the benefits of being in full connection

INTEGRATING THE CONNECTION PRACTICE INTO YOUR DAILY LIFE

In which aspects of your life do you get thrown off balance most often? Make a list of them ...

Tips for using the Connection Practice day to day:

- Ideally find a time at the beginning of the day and make the Connection Practice part of your daily routine, like brushing your teeth, showering, eating or having a cup of tea. You can download the audio version to support you with this by following the link below or scanning the QR code:

thezoneofconnection.com/downloads

- Try making the Connection Practice part of your daily routine for 21 days using this calendar (creating a habit can take longer, some sources say 30 or even 60 days of repetition)

My Daily Connection Practice Calendar

—

	Date	Time	Done (Yes or No)	Reflections
1.				
2.				
3.				
4.				
5.				
6.				

7.

8.

9.

10.

11.

12.

13.

14.

15.

16.

17.

18.

19.

20.

21.

- To begin with, practice walking around the house in this state and build up to being in it as much as possible during the day
- Experiencing everyday activities after you have expanded using the Connection Practice can make them more pleasurable
- Expand yourself using the Connection Practice in situations that you would normally find challenging
- Using the Connection Practice is particularly useful if you want to let go of something that is dominating your thoughts
- If there is a quality that you want to feel more of in your life, for example happiness, pick that quality when setting your intention at the start of the Connection Practice. Then, during the breathing sequence, you can breathe it in and, when fully expanded, get in touch with it and notice it's present in your energy field
- Start using the Fast and Instant Connection short practice audios, which you can download on the link or QR code

Your Reflections

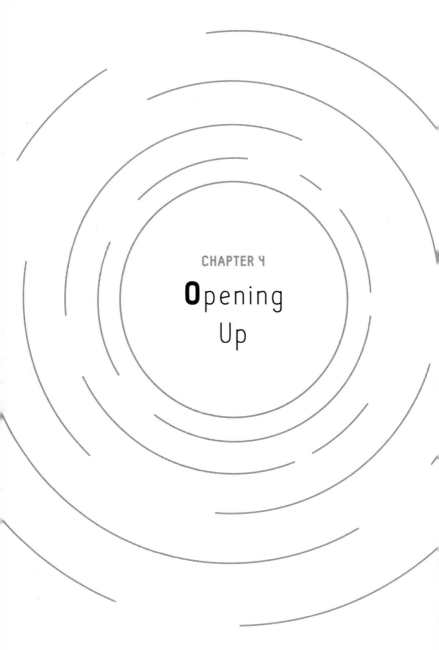

CHAPTER 4

Opening Up

"Your mind is everything: what you think is what you become."
Buddha

Core Belief: We are all a work in progress.

Possibly you find yourself *reacting* to situations rather than choosing how to respond.

Perhaps you feel held back at times by your ideas and beliefs and feel you have an inner critic controlling your life.

It could be that you sabotage your success by the stories that you tell yourself.

When we experience this way of living our lives, we feel closed, stuck, held back and frustrated.

If we are to light up our lives, what we need to create instead is a more supportive, positive approach to life that means that we are open to change, opportunity and potential. Creating this open mindset is like a flower blooming by opening its petals.

This chapter will show you how to open up to change, opportunity, potential and an abundant life through:

- Further exploration of the latest in neuroscience to understand how mindset is created
- Sharing our healing journey by installing the core beliefs that underpin an open mindset
- Demonstrating how limiting beliefs can be rewired to create a positive, empowering mindset and getting beyond the default mindset
- Exploration of energy management and the effects of stress
- Demonstrating how stress can be managed so that you are open to connecting and entering the flow of peak performance
- Sharing how blocked emotions can be liberated

This chapter includes practical exercises that you can do by downloading them using the link or QR code shared.

HOW CAN WE DEFINE MINDSET?

Sue wrote a chapter called "Mindset, Flow and Genius" with James Gairdner in *Enabling Genius* by Myles Downey. The next few paragraphs contain excerpts from this chapter.

Mindset is the neural blueprint that creates our view of the world and our way of being in the world. As shown in the diagram, mindset is multilayered. It is important to note that as we move from the outer layers toward the inner layers, we become less consciously aware of the fundamental drivers of our thoughts and behaviours.

The multilayering of mindset

—

Starting from the centre, the most unconscious parts of our mindset encompass:

- Identity – who am I?
- Purpose – why am I here?
- Values
- Attitudes and beliefs
- Talent/gifts

Much of these unconscious aspects of our mindset are hardwired during the first seven years of life, when we take on the beliefs and attitudes of those around us. Our intention sits at the interface between our internal and external worlds. This is important because it is your intention that influences the makeup of your outer (conscious) mindset and your resultant behaviours and experiences in the external world. For example, if you walk into a meeting expecting it to be hostile, you are likely to give off defensive or aggressive signals, which will provoke an equal response and, just as you predicted, a confrontational interaction.

Our feelings are our thoughts unfolding in the moment. Becoming more conscious of your intention and being able to choose it has a big influence on the feelings, thoughts, behaviours and, ultimately, outcomes you are able to achieve.

JOURNEY TO THE CENTRE OF MINDSET

The majority of us live our lives according to the default mindset acquired during our early years, unaware of the latest research in neuroscience and specifically a phenomenon called neuro-plasticity. As we said in Chapter 2, this means that our brain can continue to grow and rewire itself, enabling us to learn and grow throughout our lives. This suggests that we can update our default patterns to form new patterns of thoughts and actions in a similar way to the upgrading of software on a computer. If we stick with our default settings, we may find that they are often not appropriate for our adult lives and result in suboptimal performance.

As we mature into adulthood, we develop our self-awareness through experience, learning, feedback, reflection, coaching and, sometimes, therapy. This helps us evolve some of the outer layers, strengthening some aspects, deleting others, and adding new skills, capabilities and behavioural patterns to the mix.

Often there is a realization that some of our behaviours are not serving us well and will not enable us to get the outcomes that we want. We then learn that our thoughts and beliefs influence our emotions, and that emotions influence our behaviours (based on cognitive behavioural therapy[*]). So in order to change our behaviour we need to change our thoughts and beliefs. At this stage we start to bring some of our unconscious, limiting beliefs to conscious awareness and set about hardwiring some alternative, more empowering beliefs.

The journey through the layers of the unconscious mind can be challenging, as it requires us to let go of our existing constructs. It is then necessary to undertake an inner exploration during which you are almost held in suspense, in a kind of limbo land, where you are no longer who you were before, but nor are you who you are becoming. During this period (think caterpillar and chrysalis), you may feel lost and anxious about not knowing what the future holds. It is all about allowing the new mindset to be put in place and then the new behaviours and ways of operating in the world to emerge. Opening up to your potential means that you will constantly be growing and evolving to evermore developed levels. Thus, you go through this change – a transformation process on an ongoing basis – like an upward spiral.

Note: Cognitive Behavioural Therapy, or CBT, aims to help people become aware of negative thinking patterns and the behavioural patterns that result and to develop alternative ways of thinking and behaving that are more positive. Two of the earliest forms of cognitive behavioural therapy were Rational Emotive Behaviour Therapy (REBT), developed by Albert Ellis in the 1950s, and Cognitive Therapy, developed by Aaron T. Beck in the 1960s.

SUE'S EXPERIENCE OF CREATING
AN OPEN MINDSET

Opening up — allowing your flower to bloom

—

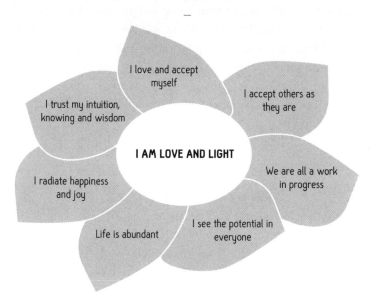

I love and accept
myself

I trust my intuition,
knowing and wisdom

I accept others as
they are

I AM LOVE AND LIGHT

I radiate happiness
and joy

We are all a work
in progress

Life is abundant

I see the potential in
everyone

I love and accept myself

When I got breast cancer in 2000, I had lost myself and gone completely out of balance. I started on a journey of getting back in touch with myself. I had counselling and coaching to support me on this journey. One of the first steps was to learn to like and even love myself again. I made this journey by looking in the mirror every day and saying, "I love and accept you exactly as you are" and being aware of how I felt.

At first, I was embarrassed to say this to myself and couldn't look myself in the eye. Gradually I got more comfortable with saying that I loved myself until finally I could say it and really mean it and, more importantly, feel it. This is the first core belief of an open mindset.

I accept others as they are

When we have aspects of ourselves that we don't like or accept, we often unconsciously project these onto other people and are judgmental and critical of them. When we love and accept ourselves, it is easier to stop being judgmental of others and accept them, even if their ways and opinions are different from ours. When others feel accepted rather than judged, they are able to be more authentic and willing to bring more of themselves to the situation. This is ongoing work for most of us. I still find that I can be judgmental of people, but I am aware of it now and use it to look at myself and ask: "Where is the part of me that is like that and do I accept it and integrate it into who I am?"

We are all a work in progress

My mother left myself and my sister when I was seven, and I believe that subconsciously I must have taken that to mean that I wasn't good enough or wasn't loveable. So I spent the next 30-odd years trying to be perfect or be the best at everything. Many of the people I coach have these limiting beliefs too – I have to be perfect (to be loved), I am not worthy of being loved, I am not good enough (to be loved) – so I am aware of the devastating impact such events and experiences can have on people's lives.

It took me quite a while to realize two things. First, that accepting yourself as you are, including your imperfections, is liberating and, second, that it doesn't mean you can't improve and grow, as we are all a work in progress. This is what it means to live from a growth mindset as opposed to a fixed mindset (see Carol S. Dweck's book, *Mindset*).

I see the potential in everyone

This leads to the next core belief, that we all have unlimited potential should we choose to realize it. I am a learning junky and love to grow and learn new things. Many people are afraid to grow and try new things in case they fail. When we ask people to think of those who had the most impact on their lives, it is usually someone who believed in them more than they did themselves, thus giving them the confidence to do things they never dreamt they were capable of.

From my work as a coach I know that when you have this attitude toward people they grow in confidence and absolutely blossom. How you see people is how they show up, so seeing the potential in them helps them to step into it. This starts with how you see yourself. You can't see unlimited potential in others if you don't first see it in yourself.

Life is abundant

I was brought up by my dad, who had a scarcity mindset. He worked all hours because he had a fear of not having enough money. I found that I took this on and as a young adult I was afraid of not being able to support myself. I, too, worked long hours and tried to be the best at everything. Eventually I burnt out and got cancer.

I now realize that the universe is abundant and that there is plenty of success to go around. I don't have to compete and grab more than my share of success; instead I can relax in knowing that I will always be able to earn what I need.

I radiate happiness and joy

Given my previous mindset, it will come as no surprise that I believed that happiness came from obtaining material wealth and possessions. This fed into my scarcity mentality and caused me to work hard to earn as much money as possible so that I could have the big house and nice car, and that those things would make me feel happy.

Of course, when I got those things the happiness was short-lived. I now know that happiness is something that is on the inside. It comes from loving ourselves and wanting to make a difference in the world by serving others. People who are innately happy radiate that feeling out into the world. Others gravitate toward them as they catch their happiness vibe.

I trust my intuition, knowing and wisdom

When I found out that I had cancer, I spent most of the time in my head. I allowed my thoughts to dictate my life and used rational thinking to make my decisions, often overthinking them. I felt that I could make things happen if I put my mind to it.

Gradually, as I got more in touch with my body and my feelings, my intuition started to kick in and eventually I learned to trust it. I realized I had innate abilities of sensing and knowing, and I learned how to connect with them and use them to influence my choices in life. As I grew and developed further, I was able to tap into my deep wisdom and speak it when needed. Accessing all of these sources of intelligence enables me to trust myself and allow my life to flow, as opposed to striving and forcing things to happen.

I was able to do all of this by practising the Connection Practice we developed and shared with you in the previous chapter.

I am love and light

The journey of self-discovery after having found that I had cancer was like having a love affair with myself. Eventually I arrived at the deepest level of the journey and started to explore my identity. This helped me to see that we are all energy and that the energy that we are all made of is a universal love energy. I came to believe that we are all made of love at our core. Once we begin to live life knowing this, we can truly start to shine our light into the world and radiate that love.

These are the beliefs that create an open mindset. My journey has been a wonderful one; it never really ends, as there are always new opportunities to consciously live these beliefs day to day.

HOW TO REWIRE BELIEFS

There are four aspects that develop our negative or limiting beliefs:
- During our early years we have experiences that create our ideas about 'self', such as rejection, neglect or being the 'odd one out', which lead to …
- Our core belief. This is an assessment of our worth or value as a person, which may lead to other beliefs such as "I am worthless" or "I am not good enough"
- These develop our guidelines for coping or survival – "I must avoid this," "I must always put others first," "if I am myself I will be rejected" – which lead to …
- Trigger situations. These are situations in which our guidelines are transgressed, resulting in defensiveness and feelings of rejection, failure or being out of control

So, your early experiences, and the limiting beliefs they create, not only remain unchallenged into adulthood, but also generate self-reinforcing and self-fulfilling mechanisms that are regularly triggered.

What then happens is that your brain filters the information it receives to find things that confirm your hardwired beliefs. These beliefs become your thoughts and your inner dialogue, which influence how you feel, what you do and the outcomes you get as a result. It becomes a self-fulfilling prophecy, which is not easy to break out of.

The reason is that your brain likes certainty; it likes to maintain the status quo and does not like change. So, you tend to hold onto your hardwired view of the world for fear that if you change it, your world may collapse. What this means is that, in a world that is constantly and rapidly changing, your view of the world very quickly becomes outdated and holds you back or keeps you stuck. You are not taught about the need to regularly scan your beliefs and update those that are no longer aligned with the outcomes that you want. You don't realize that you need to update your software. But it is important to do so, and it can be achieved by using the process of neuroplasticity (discussed in Chapter 2) to rewire your brain and update your software. Learning how to let go of beliefs that hold you back is an important life skill.

The first step is to bring these limiting beliefs to conscious awareness so that you become aware of them as they arise in the moment. Since these beliefs have been in place for so long, throughout your life, they are buried deep in your subconscious, and it takes patience and skill to bring them to the surface. Using the Connection Practice heightens your awareness. It does this by helping you to slow down and be present in the moment so that you can notice what is going on inside you. You might not initially be able to articulate the belief, but you are aware of how you are feeling and what sensations happen in your body as you start to react based on your subconscious beliefs. The Connection Practice facilitates the process of identifying the limiting beliefs that are holding you back.

Once you have identified your limiting beliefs, you can start to identify a more empowering set of new beliefs given the outcomes you want to bring about.

Neuroscience shows that you can't just overwrite these existing beliefs, which are hardwired into neural pathways in your subconscious brain. The only way is to create new neural pathways for the new beliefs that you identify, using the neuroplasticity of your brain. This means that you control your own reality, because you can change your thoughts, beliefs and mindset.

Essentially your brain plays a big part in determining your state of mind and your reactions. If you are consumed by negative beliefs and negative mindsets, you are likely to be less happy than people with a generally positive set of beliefs. When you have positive beliefs, you create more dopamine and serotonin, the feel-good chemicals in the brain. These chemicals are electrical transmitters and allow your brain not only to process optimally but also to support the neuroplasticity you need to rewire your limiting beliefs. Essentially, your brain's influence on whether you feel happy and positive goes well beyond beliefs.

Your brain changes frequencies at different times during the day and these different frequencies heavily influence your state of mind, as each frequency puts you into a different state of consciousness. There are five main brainwave frequencies as we explored in Chapter 2: beta, alpha, theta, delta and gamma.

When your hardwired beliefs were installed during the early years of your life, your brain was vibrating at a theta frequency. In order to hardwire a new behaviour, we need to get access to the subconscious mind and encourage it to create a new neural pathway. This can be done by accessing the theta state and going direct to the subconscious using hypnotherapy or meditation.

Other ways of creating new neural pathways are lengthier and require more effort. Over time you would need to focus on the new belief such that your subconscious decides to hardwire and embed it. There are a number of possible ways to do this, which involve thinking about it, speaking about it (possibly using positive statements and affirmations) and practising the new behaviour. With this method, it is best to think about the new beliefs that you want to hardwire when you are just about to go to sleep or when you are waking up, because your brain is in a receptive state at these times.

However, the Connection Practice switches you to a lower frequency, such as alpha or theta. By doing so, you will have more awareness of your limiting beliefs and also enter a state where your subconscious is receptive to the new beliefs that you create in this state.

START TO REWIRE YOUR
LIMITING BELIEFS

Limiting beliefs are often deeply buried. The following exercise may help to bring them to the surface. If this doesn't work, you may need to get the help of a coach or healing practitioner.

Exercise 5
Rewiring limiting beliefs

Step 1: Relive the situation

o Think of a situation in the recent past when you felt uncomfortable, blocked or stuck, or you overreacted

o Close your eyes, picture the scene and relive it as fully as possible. What is happening around you? What are people saying? What are you doing? What are you saying/not saying? How do you feel?

o Write down verbatim everything that was running in your head at the time. Don't censor it: just write what is there

Step 2: Identify the belief

Limiting beliefs often start with 'I must', 'I should', or 'I can't'. Here are some examples:

o I must be perfect to be loved/worthwhile, etc.

o I must be right

o I'm not good enough

o I must work hard to prove I'm good enough

o If I make a mistake, others will ridicule me and think I am no good

o If I challenge others or express a different opinion, others won't like me

Next you can start to tackle your own beliefs:

o Look at what you wrote down in Step 1, highlight any limiting beliefs and write them down in a list

o Take each limiting belief and say, "What would that mean to me?"

o Keep repeating this question until you get to the underlying limiting belief

Sometimes we have faulty thinking patterns that hold us back — see if you relate to any of those set out in the following table.

Faulty thinking patterns

—

Distortion	Meaning
Discounting the positive	*If I can do it, it doesn't count.*
All-or-nothing thinking	*I pass or I fail.. Or, I'll do it all now or not do it at all.*
Labelling	*I did something bad; therefore, I am bad.*
Mind-reading	*She didn't look at me, therefore I must have done something wrong.*
Fortune-telling	*I just know it will be awful.*
Catastrophizing	*OMG this is SOOOO terrible.*
Personalization	*It's all my fault.*
Blame	*It's all their fault.*
Generalization	*Things never go right for me.*
Should, must, have to, ought to	*I/you/he/she should ... must ... have to ... ought to ...*

Step 3: Tune into feelings

○ For the limiting beliefs that you have identified, take a note of the experiences in your body and your feelings as you recall the times when this limiting belief held you back

○ You may re-experience feelings that you had at the time – this shows the strong connection between thinking and feeling

Step 4: Check for assumptions

○ Read through each limiting belief and ask yourself whether it is a fact or an assumption – anything that predicts an outcome in the future is an assumption

○ Ask yourself what it is costing you to continue with this assumption

○ Look critically at each belief. Is it really true?

Step 5: Reframe the situation

○ Reframe every assumption into a belief that will support you better or one that is more empowering

○ Identify a positive reframe for every negative belief, such as:
  If I speak out, I will get conflict.

Positive reframe:
  If I assert my view, they will listen. If I do get into conflict, I can both listen to them and stand my ground.

Step 6: Visualize the outcome

Use the Connection Practice to get your mind into a relaxed, creative and receptive state:

○ Set your intention to identify beliefs that will support and empower you

○ Feel your feet on the ground and your spine aligned

○ Close your eyes

○ Notice the sensations in your body and take a moment to relax

○ Bring your attention to the energy surrounding your body and feel for balance

○ Take a big breath and let go of anything you don't need right here by sighing it out. This includes those limiting beliefs you have identified

○ Breathe in from your head down through your heart to your gut, connecting yourself up

○ Take another of these long conscious breaths down into your belly as you slow down and become calmer

○ From the centre of your chest, start to imagine a line going up through your body and all the way to the centre of the radiant sun

○ Enjoy the warmth of the sun's energy for a few moments

○ Now come back down the line into your body and down to the earth, all the way to the earth's molten core

○ Take a moment to feel your source energy and to feel grounded with the earth

○ Feel aligned between the sun and the earth

○ Sense the energy in your heart opening and expanding into your entire body

○ Allow this energy to continue to expand beyond your body

○ As the energy expands outside of your body, feel the energy merging with the energy around you, feel the energy getting bigger and bigger

○ Allow the vibrant energy to continue to expand way out to encompass the whole earth, out past the planets, and connect to the infinite universe

○ Expand out as far as you can possibly imagine, to where you have no edges and are fully connected to everything in the entire universe

○ From this expanded state, imagine a situation when you noticed your limiting beliefs coming into play in the past. This time imagine a positive outcome happening based on your new positive belief

With time, as you use the Connection Practice in this way, you will gradually see a positive outcome from similar situations. You will start to notice how you are dealing with such situations differently.

Step 7: Embedding the new beliefs

Changing beliefs and habitual behaviours takes time, as you have to create a new neural pathway. This happens if the behaviour or thought is repeated/focused on often enough.

Each time you notice the old limiting belief coming into play, pause and use the Connection Practice to connect up. You will create a six- to ten-second gap in which you can consciously change it to your new positive belief.

This won't happen immediately. It takes time and you might need to ask someone to encourage you when they see the new behaviour and remind you if they see you lapsing back into the old behaviour.

One way of embedding your new positive supportive beliefs is to use them as affirmations. The idea is to repeat these affirmations (you should not have too many, ideally) to yourself every night when you are half asleep or every morning when you are half awake — this is when your subconscious mind is most accessible. It takes sustained effort, but eventually you will realize that you are operating to the new set of beliefs.

An important and effective addition is the use of visualization, a powerful technique used in sports. This works through our mirror neurons, which cause us to mimic things. We create pictures in our minds and mimic them, and we also mimic others. If we visualize how we want to be and if, when doing our affirmations, we replay these images as if they are actually happening, then we can consciously choose to make this our reality. As we go through this process, we take back control because we are choosing what is in our subconscious. We put it there, we wrote the program.

As these new beliefs start to influence your behaviours, there will be times when you lapse back into the old behaviours. It is important to realize that the thoughts in our minds are making our decisions six to ten seconds before we are aware of what we are going to do. The Connection Practice will make you become more present in the moment and aware of your behaviours. You will notice these choices and take a pause to consciously select the new behaviour as opposed to allowing the old one to automatically happen. In this way you begin to gain the ability to make your own choices and stop the previously embedded automatic responses. This begins to change the programming in your subconscious.

STRESS - DON'T LET IT
CLOSE YOU DOWN

Another key aspect of opening up and living from the ZOC is being able to handle stress. All of us experience stress from time to time and a certain amount of positive stress (eustress) motivates us, but too much negative stress has a detrimental impact on our lives.

The brain is wired to sense danger and provide the appropriate stress response from fight/flight/freeze to help us survive the impending danger. To have the energy to run or fight, the brain shuts down the prefrontal cortex, which is the executive centre where our short-term memory is and where all of our best thinking and planning is done. (The activity of the prefrontal cortex includes energy-hungry mental processes such as understanding information, making decisions, recalling existing information, memorizing and storing new information, and prioritizing.) This completely disables us from operating effectively and results in a very narrow focus on the perceived danger with our mind closed to everything else. This embedded behaviour focuses on what we don't want to happen and prepares us for the worst thing that could possibly happen.

Additionaly, stress hormones such as cortisol and adrenaline are released into our system. These are all right in short bursts, but as many of us are operating in a stressful state for extended periods, the ongoing presence of these hormones in the body can cause health problems such as anxiety, depression, headaches, digestive problems, heart disease, weight gain, memory and concentration impairment, and sleep problems. On top of all this, these chemicals are electrical inhibitors and prevent the brain from working optimally and from creating new neural pathways or rewiring.

Chronic stress results in our muscles forgetting how to relax. Our muscles need to be able to relax to allow blood to flow sufficiently through our bodies in order to move oxygen in and toxins out.

Learning how to manage your personal energy is a key part of managing stress effectively (see Tony Schwartz and Jim Loehr's book, *The Power of Full Engagement: Managing Energy Not Time*). When we talk about personal energy management, we talk about four energy zones: the ZOC or Peak Performance Zone; the Survival or Stress Zone; the Burn-Out Zone and the Recovery Zone, as shown in the following table.

Personal energy management

—

Survival/Stress Zone	Zone of Connection (ZOC)/ Peak Performance Zone
Frustration	Centred
	Happy
Anxiety	Present
	Effortless
Anger	Alive
	Powerful
Fear	Creative
	Flow
Irritation	Energized
	Inspired
Unbalanced	Balanced
Burn-Out Zone	**Recovery Zone**
Exhausted	Relaxed
Apathetic	Peaceful
Listless	Calm
Dis-ease	Still
Lifeless	At ease
Helpless	In your body

Imagine a time when you are at your best, in a state of flow – how do you feel? What percentage of the time are you there? This is when you are in the ZOC and here you can reach peak performance. In the ZOC, you have a broader perspective, you are open to change and challenges, you feel valued and confident, you feel at ease and things flow better in your life. The adjectives in the table are often used to describe the feelings people experience when they are in the ZOC. So, ideally, you want to spend more time in this zone, where you experience more of these positive emotions.

Looking at the recovery zone, think about what you do to recover emotionally during the day. What does it feel like to be in the recovery zone? The process of recovery and re-energizing helps you to build energy and resistance to when things get really bad. If you are not giving yourself time during the day to recover and re-energize, your relationships may suffer and your brain struggles to remain creative. Through using the Connection Practice, you can get into the recovery zone and re-energize to find the still, calm centre in you.

When demands exceed your capacity, the energy going out from you is more than that which is coming in, so you enter the survival zone and present a stress response.

What percentage of time are you in the survival zone? How do you feel when you are in this zone? People often describe this feeling with negative emotions.

By constantly being in the survival zone you are in danger of going into the burn-out zone. Not a pleasant place to be. The feelings you experience in this zone are definitely ones you want to avoid.

The Connection Practice will help you to avoid this as it enables you to enter the ZOC and experience peak performance or flow. Flow is an energetic state that you can learn to step into by using the Connection Practice. Being in this state gives you the opportunity to live your life more fully. This state of flow is not easy to put into words, but it can be thought of as those moments when you feel still inside, effortless, everything feels just right, at peace, but you are also alert and attentive, exhilarated by life and fully alive. The mind, body and spirit are in sync.

A state of flow in individuals enables the highest levels of performance to emerge by unleashing potential, creativity, and feelings of confidence and wellbeing. To access a state of flow, you have to learn to slow down, feel a sense of spaciousness, to be present in the moment, centred and grounded inside, undisturbed by what is going on the outside. From there you can expand and tap into all the potential that is available.

When you open up to your potential and are managing your energy better – so that you avoid being closed down by the stress response – you can access flow and experience improved self-esteem, confidence, resilience, balance, better mental and physical health, making better choices, greater productivity, and a healthy mind, body and spirit.

INTERRUPTING THE STRESS RESPONSE

In the Stress or Survival Zone, you are in the stress response of fight/flight/freeze as described in Chapter 2. The stress response takes over and your thinking brain is shut down, resulting in impaired functioning. How do you switch from that default operating system to one where you consciously choose how to respond?

Default stress-creating operating system

—

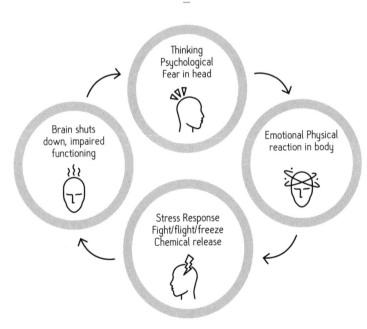

Fortunately, you also have a direct response network, the *full-connection operating system*. This system uses the multi-brain to take in information from all of your senses and the environment in real time.

Interruption of stress response:
the full-connection operating system

—

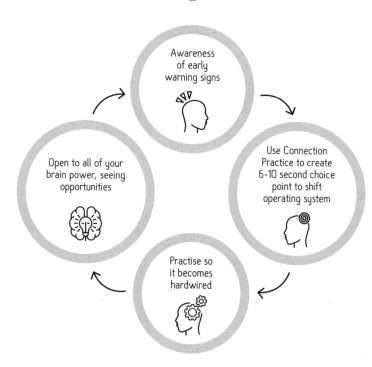

In this mode, you are able to observe by standing back from your thoughts and getting closer to the reality of what is happening in the moment. Therefore, you respond more flexibly to the events that unfold (see David Rock's book, *Your Brain at Work*).

First, you notice the early warning signals – your thoughts, emotions and your body's reactions. These tell you that you are about to go into the stress response. We know from neuroscience that you have a six- to ten-second gap in which to interrupt the default reaction and choose a different response before you are completely taken over. Making the conscious choice to use the Connection Practice during this six- to ten-second gap, you interrupt the stress response and can switch to the full-connection operating system.

By repeating this process, you create new neural pathways, rewiring your brain until this is hardwired and you can switch at will between these operating systems. This opens you up to your true power, where you can see the opportunities and potential from a greater perspective in every situation.

Using the Instant Connection Practice to interrupt the stress response

We have created a bonus exercise that guides you through the process of using the Instant Connection Practice to interrupt the stress response and break out of this automatic reaction so that you can choose the most appropriate response for the situation. It is available to download on the link below or scanning the QR code:

thezoneofconnection.com/bonuses

LIBERATING BLOCKED EMOTIONS

Blocked emotions from the past can stop you from accessing the ZOC.

Most of the time, the emotions that you generate in response to an external event deliver a message to the brain and continue to pass through your body. However, sometimes external events cause reactions that evoke fear or anxiety and you resist these emotions, or in the opposite case you like the associated feelings and cling on to the emotions. In both cases you are not letting the emotions pass through because you are blocking the flow. Clinging means that you don't want this to go away, that you want to keep reliving that moment. An example of clinging would be an emotion that brings you sympathy or attention. These behaviours develop during childhood to please carers and get attention, but when established they keep you responding as a child rather than a responsible, accountable adult.

When this happens, you fixate on the experiences that enable energy patterns to get stuck. As a result, life cannot flow freely and must compete with this blocked event for your attention. You will constantly think about the blocked event in an attempt to find a way to process it through your mind. Thought after thought continues inside your mind, driving you crazy. When energy can't make it through the mind because of conflicts with other thoughts and mental concepts, it then tries to release through the heart. All that inner noise is your attempt to process the blocked energy and remove it. That is what creates all the emotional activity.

When you resist releasing such energy, there is no other place for it to go and it will continue to circulate inside you. Eventually these circulating energy packets are stored in your body and become inactive energy blocks – your programming. By the time you reach adulthood, you have so many unresolved experiences that many of your responses are automatically negative, and you are caught in a negative emotional cycle often based on the long-forgotten past.

Eventually this blocked energy builds up and restricts energy flow through your energy centres. If this builds up sufficiently, you will find yourself in a state of depression or suffering from physical illness. These unresolved stored energy patterns end up running your life and, worryingly, they may be stored for a very long time. Additionally, you may sometimes – unconsciously – project your buried negative emotions onto other people, which will have a negative effect on your relationships.

This habit of avoiding and blocking emotions is one of the main causes of a whole range of psychological problems. Have you ever avoided difficult emotions only to find that even more pain builds up at a later stage? Doing this is like a person under stress drinking alcohol to relieve their pain. The alcohol blocks out the feelings and emotions in the short term and makes them feel better. But the next time they feel stressed, they drink again. Eventually they develop a bigger problem, an addiction to alcohol, all without resolving the issues causing the stress in the first place.

What happens when these blocked emotions get triggered?

At some point the flow of current thoughts and events causes the stored energy to be activated or triggered – possibly years later. This is what happens when you feel under duress. Reactions that trigger blocked emotions include feeling judged by others, feeling that you're a victim or comparing yourself negatively to others.

When a stored pattern gets stimulated, it begins to release the stored energy. It is as if a stagnant, festering pool of energy begins to flow again. Suddenly flashes of what you experienced when the original event took place rush into your consciousness – the thoughts, the feelings, sometimes even the smells and other sensory input. As these unfinished mental and emotional energy patterns are reactivated, you can feel the fears and insecurity you felt as a child. This stops you from being present in the moment and responding with clarity. You know you have been triggered when your reaction is out of proportion to the current situation. But each time blocked emotions are triggered, it is an opportunity to see the old pattern, process it and let go of it.

You will get to a point in your growth where you will understand that if you close down and protect yourself, you will never be free. You will never grow and realize your potential when you protect stored issues. Living like that doesn't allow life to flow and, as a result, you experience very little spontaneous joy, enthusiasm and excitement. You see life as a threat and a good day means you got through without getting hurt. But life should be seen as a journey where you use the opportunities thrown at you to heal and grow.

Use the Connection Practice to let go of blocked emotions.

Eventually, as you use the Connection Practice to stay centred and open, you will be able to shift your blocked emotions and stored energy patterns. Although they will continue to come up, you will have the ability to automatically let them go by staying centred and letting go of the energy, so that they pass straight through you. Just like the physical body purges bacteria and foreign matter, the natural flow of your energy will purge the stored negative emotions from your energy centres. Your reward will be a permanently open inner channel through which your energy can flow freely. Use Exercise 6 to support you with this.

Exercise 6
Letting go of blocked emotions

First, find a place where you will not be disturbed.

○ Create a safe space for yourself, where you are noticing but not judging. Just be yourself. There is no right or wrong experience; whatever you feel is just right for you. Have an open mind and be playful and willing to experiment, have fun and let go of past learning

○ Really going for this will help you to get the most out of it. Do it in a way that works for you, so if you are asked to stand up and you are uncomfortable, please feel free to do it sitting down

○ There may be some language you haven't heard or seen before – just trust the process, trust yourself and trust us!

Go for it! It will have a transformational effect on your life and others too.

Step 1: Setting Intentions

○ Close your eyes and start to tune into any area of your life where you have experienced negative emotions. It might be an area where you feel blocked, where you don't feel good, or where you feel stressed or fearful. Take a moment to bring to mind a time when you have felt like that

○ Set an intention to shift any blocked emotions. Imagine that amazing possibility for yourself right there in front of you and say YES to it

Step 2: Use the Connection Practice
to let go of blocked emotions

Posture and balance is important here, as your body functions best when you are aligned whether standing, seated or lying down.

○ Lengthen your spine and open your chest, feel a posture of uprightness, feeling supported with a sense of integrity and alignment

○ Relax your jaw and shoulders – let gravity have them

○ Soften your heart and relax your pelvic floor

○ Start to allow yourself to become aware of what's going on for you right now in this moment

○ Take a moment to observe what is going on in your thoughts, your feelings and your body, and notice any sensations with a sense of acceptance

Extending beyond your physical body is your energy body, which is the sphere of energy that surrounds you. You are now going to feel for balance within your energy body.

○ Repeat the statement: "I allow myself to wonder, what would it be like if my energy was equal and even at the back and front of my body?"

○ If it helps, you can imagine your energy field as a colour or texture. If the energy field was equal and even to the right and left sides? And if the energy field was equal and even above your head and below your body?

○ Take a moment to feel for that balance. Allow yourself to rest in the safety of your field and trust it to support you

○ Call upon your awareness to notice your breath. Take a moment to notice where it is in your body

○ Now bring to mind the negative energy that has felt blocked, tune back into it, remember when you last felt it

○ Feel where it is in your body. What does it feel like — colour, texture, image?

○ Notice it, acknowledge it and give yourself permission to let it go

○ Start by taking some big breaths in through your nose then sighing out through your mouth

○ Really let yourself feel this energy, breathe into it and then breathe it out. If sounds need to come as you do this, just let them come

○ Let go of anything that is blocking you, breathe it out; keep letting go, coming back to who you really are

Do this cleansing breath a few times. Really let all that blocked emotion go.

Now use your breath to become really present by continuing the practice:

- Inhale for a count of six, pause until your body naturally wants to breathe out and exhale for a count of six
- As you breathe in slowly and fully through your nose, allow your belly to expand. The belly is the seat of your sense of presence, knowing and deep confidence. Breathe your energy down from your head into your heart and gut brain to connect all of yourself up
- Repeat this breathing technique two more times
- Feel yourself calming down and a sense of stillness, allowing everything to be as it is
- Notice how you feel now that you have shifted those blocked emotions. Give yourself a beautiful inner smile

In short
KEY CONCEPTS ON OPENING UP

- In order to change your behaviour, you need to change your thoughts and beliefs
- In the theta state, your brain is receptive and can more easily be rewired. The Connection Practice helps you to access this state
- Stress stops your brain from functioning and makes you feel negatively. Interrupting the stress response and other automatic reactions using the Connection Practice creates a six- to ten-second gap in which you can choose how to respond

INTEGRATING AN OPEN MINDSET INTO YOUR DAILY LIFE

- Use Exercise 5 in this chapter (page 99) to surface limiting beliefs and replace them with positive, empowering beliefs
- Use Exercise 6 in this chapter (page 115) to let go of blocked emotions
- If you find yourself being held back by stress, follow the bonus exercise (page 111) to download and learn how to interrupt that pattern

Trying it out for yourself! What are the first steps you intend to take to develop an open mindset? Write them down.

Your Reflections

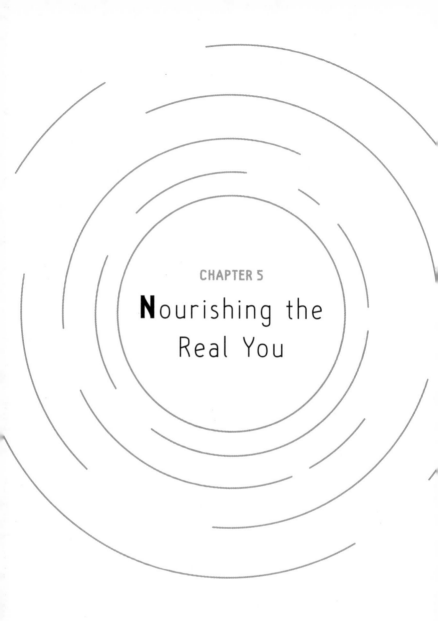

CHAPTER 5

Nourishing the Real You

"Success in any endeavour depends on the degree
to which it is an expression of your true self."
Ralph Marston

Core Belief: I love and accept myself.

Perhaps you judge yourself and sometimes compare yourself to others. Maybe you play small through a fear of failing. Possibly you try to be the person you think others want you to be.

Accepting yourself for who you are and seeing your authentic self enables you to feel relaxed and enjoy who you really are. Authenticity creates trust. You trust in yourself and others trust you. Love starts with yourself, so it is important that you live your life through the lens of seeing yourself for who you really are.

Everything in life begins with connection. Everything we do, and every relationship we have, succeeds or fails based on our level of true connection. To connect with others and have the greatest potential for peace and joy, you must learn to connect first with yourself.

Everything you want in any relationship begins inside you – with how much love, understanding and forgiveness you have for yourself. You cannot receive what you cannot give. When you try to create relationships from the outside in, you put the burden on external approval, success, money and getting what you want. You look for a person who fits your long list of wants, when the reality is everything is happening from the inside out. The situation out there reflects the situation in here. With regular use of the Connection Practice, you get familiar with your inner self and your energetic landscape, and you will be able to experience yourself for who you really are.

Working from the outside in will fall short of the ideal, and leads to frustration, conflict and lack of fulfilment in the end. If you try to base your relationships on your small ego self, you are in a disconnected and unaware state, and you can easily feel like a victim when things get difficult. You then start to blame yourself and feel that when things go wrong it is your fault. This sounds like it is taking responsibility, but it's not. That is the inner voice of victimization.

When you live life from a fully connected place, you feel strong and dynamic. From this state, you can discover who you really are. Essentially, a new identity is being created, which is the foundation for good connection with others and being in your true power.

We can choose to connect with another person or not, but we cannot choose to disconnect from ourselves. Many people are uncomfortable with this truth – they spend vast amounts of time escaping from themselves with all kinds of activities, work and distractions. So, bringing relationships back to the self can sound scary or difficult. It is a beautiful ideal to envision a relationship with yourself that solves all other relationships.

But is it realistic? The answer for countless people is that it's not. In the beginning, all of us have self-centred tastes, aims, desires, opinions, likes and dislikes – because from the beginning our sense of self is ego-based. The very construct of the ego brings with it a built-in conflict with other egos. If you think about it, it is surprising that egos, each with their own rules and agendas, can ever get together in the first place. When they do, there is always a risk of the connection unravelling because the ego is primarily tied to what it wants.

The path to an ideal relationship, therefore, must get past the ego with its insecurities, demands and endless focus on 'I', 'me' and 'mine'.

You can go beyond the ego by accessing a fully connected state. In this state you feel at peace, secure, safe, cared for and, most of all, happy. This is what is sometimes referred to as your true or real self. It is a state of awareness –not a thing, mood, sensation or feeling.

So when you feel disconnected, this is an indication that there is a gap between the self you imagine yourself to be and the self you really are.

Nourishing your authentic self is about learning to love yourself and like your own company. Many of us have a fear of loneliness. It is about knowing that you are never alone and that you already have all of what you need to be happy inside. When you find out who you really are, you realize that nothing else is needed beyond that. This allows you to reveal your most radiant, magnificent self and light up your life.

Sue's wake-up call around this came in 2000 with her breast cancer diagnosis.

SUE'S EXPERIENCE OF LEARNING TO LOVE HERSELF

I went to the Bristol Cancer Centre to learn about how to use complementary therapies and diet to support me during my treatment. The holistic doctor there asked me what percentage of my energy was focused on my mind, what percentage on my body and what percentage on my spirit. My answer was 95% mind, 5% body and spirit, what is that? I realized how out of balance I had become and that I had disconnected from myself and lost myself. As I said in Chapter 4, Opening Up, since then I have been on a journey that has largely been about having a love affair with myself, and it has been a fantastic journey.

Why did my journey start with focusing on my relationship with myself? The quality of your relationship with yourself determines the quality of your relationship with everything else. It influences your physical wellbeing, your food choices, the exercise you get, and your relationship with money. It influences your emotional wellbeing, the pace you set for your life, the time you make for yourself and how loveable you feel. It also influences your spiritual wellbeing, your creativity and how happy you are. The better you get on with yourself, the better life gets.

Why? Quantum science shows that everything is energy and all energy is interconnected and that separation is not real. Therefore, your relationship with yourself affects every other relationship in your life. Your capacity to love yourself influences how much you let yourself be loved by others. When you feel loveable, you don't need to put on a pleasing image to win love, you don't need to do things in order to deserve love. You let love in. You are a good receiver.

When I started my journey following the visit to Bristol Cancer Centre, I thought that self-love was the same as self-care and what you do for yourself. It took me a long time to realize that it is much more than that, that it is an inner journey. The start of that realization for me was to start to love my physical appearance and to stop judging and criticizing myself, thereby making myself feel that I was not loveable. It is about having a positive self-image and positive beliefs about yourself. It's about enjoying your own company and being connected to your whole being, listening to your body, to your intuition and wisdom, and trusting it. It is about the essence of who you are. I can now look in the mirror and truly feel that unconditional love for myself.

Eventually I came to believe that we start life as unconditional love and our journey through life is to get back to that again. However, what I now know is that it is not something you search for on the outside, but rather it is already there on the inside, something that we come back to. If unconditional love is our original energy, then our essence or true self is founded on unconditional love.

How do you access the ability to see and experience who you really are?

You can do this by accessing all of your intelligence and not just focusing on your rational, head-based intelligence. Many people fear not knowing and try to control every aspect of their lives from their head brain. The good news is that we were born with innate abilities that come into play here. The problem is we may not access them as readily and as often as we could. Once you are aware of and trust your innate abilities, there is no fear. You can never not know!

SO, WHAT ARE THESE INNATE ABILITIES?

Innate abilities are three natural abilities that we are born with: intuition, sensing and knowing. Over time and with the tendency to live through our heads and default operating system, we are not consciously aware of this aspect of our intelligence. We often ignore it, not trusting the information and guidance that it offers us.

Intuition

We're all aware that we have intuition. So, what is it? It's a 'gut-feel' – that quick feeling, that immediate sensing that something is right or wrong.

Sensing

This is where we use our senses and sensors to feel what's going on around us. Have you ever walked into a beautiful place and felt a deep sense of peace?

Have you ever sensed that it's going to be one of those days on your way to work? That's innate sensing. You're tuning into what is happening in that environment, even before you're physically in it. You are using a sixth sense that goes beyond your five traditional senses. What you are tuning into is energy, and energy is subtle. It's like a radio signal that you are tuning into; you can't see, hear, smell, taste, or touch energy.

Knowing

Have you ever been in a challenging situation, probably one that you are experiencing for the first time, and know exactly what you need to do or say in that moment? Afterwards you might say to yourself, "Where did that come from?"

When you shift from autopilot to a fully connected state using the Connection Practice, you are able to access the innate ability of knowing.

What is knowing? This is the ability to accept that everything is energy and that you can connect with that energy, and you can access knowledge and understanding from this connection. Some people say that it is as if your mind is a computer; it is plugged into the internet and can download from a source of unlimited information. Receiving this information takes you into different forms of awareness that are usually not rational, fully formed sentences! For example, you might see an image, feel a sensation, get a word, colours or symbols, and through trusting this information are able to understand and get guidance from it. In this way, you are accessing your wisdom and what we call a quantum level of intelligence.

What if everything we want to know is there and available for us to access right now, and we can do so at the flick of a switch? Your true self lives beyond what you know with your rational mind and enables you to connect to everything.

Penny has some hereditary deafness. When she started to understand innate abilities, she realized that having one sense impaired had made it somehow easier for her to get beyond the five senses and that she had always used these natural innate abilities to tune into and know what was going on.

Using the Connection Practice, you can integrate your head, heart and gut brains, access your fully connected operating system, and use your amazing innate sensing and knowing to connect with your authentic self, the real you.

Use the Connection Practice to bond with the real you and express your personal frequency.

There are three exercises in this chapter to support you in putting what you learn into practice. The best way to experience them is by being guided by us using the audio version, which you can download using the link or QR code shared. Alternatively, you can do them by recording them on your phone and playing them back or by using the explanation in the text.

In Exercise 7 you use the Connection Practice to access your fully connected operating system and use your amazing innate sensing and knowing to connect with your authentic self, the real you.

Exercise 7
Connecting with the real you
using innate abilities

○ Set an intention to use your knowing to connect with your true, authentic self, to experience your love and compassion for yourself, and to accept your uniqueness

○ Feel your feet on the ground and your spine aligned

○ Close your eyes

○ Notice any sensations in your body and take a moment to allow it to relax

○ Bring your attention to the energy surrounding your body and feel for balance in it

○ Take a big breath in and as you sigh your breath out, let go of anything that gets in the way of connecting with your true self. Next time you breathe in, imagine breathing in love and sighing out anything that stops love energy flowing within you. Imagine as you take these deep breaths that you are bathing your cells in the love energy you have been breathing in. Repeat this a few times

○ Now take a few long conscious breaths down into your belly as you slow down and become calmer

○ From the centre point in your chest, start to imagine a line going up through your body and all the way to the centre of the radiant sun

○ Now come back down the line into your body and down to the earth, all the way to the earth's molten core, your source energy, feeling grounded

○ Feel aligned between the sun and the earth

○ Sense the energy in your heart centre starting to open, ready for a relationship with the real you. See the energy expand into your body

○ Allow this energy to expand beyond your body, merging with the energy around you, getting bigger and bigger

○ Expand that vibrant energy way out to encompass the whole earth out past the planets and connecting to the infinite universe

- Expand out as far as you can possibly imagine, to where you have no edges and are fully connected to everything
- From this expanded state, imagine that your authentic self is sitting opposite. You see him/her as a fully expanded and connected enormous energy being. Imagine that you are connected by a field of unconditional love. Now imagine that you are tuning into that amazing being opposite, just like you tune into the frequency of a radio station. Once you are tuned in on the right frequency ask your true self to reveal itself to you
- Let the pictures, colours, feelings, symbols, sensations just come to you to give you clues as to who you really are and what your contribution/potential is
- Allow the answers to come into your knowing (often they come in through your gut). Be patient and trust without judgment whatever comes
- When you sense you have received all of the knowing, open your eyes and allow yourself to express what has come to you. You can do this by writing it down, speaking it and recording it, or drawing or painting it
- When you have finished, sit with what has come to you and allow any further insights and awareness to emerge. Feel the vibration of this knowing about the real you in your body
- Continue with this until you feel all the information has been revealed to you

We all vibrate at a unique personal vibrational frequency or signature vibe. This is the manifestation of who we really are, and others can pick up on this. In the next exercise, we will again use the Connection Practice so that you integrate your head, heart and gut brains and access your fully connected operating system. This time you are going to use full connection to tune into your personal frequency. When a frequency is vibrating fast enough, it can be emitted as a sound, so in this exercise you will experience your personal frequency through sound.

Exercise 8
Expressing your personal vibrational frequency or signature vibe

○ Set an intention to expand to Full Connection and from there experience your signature vibe and sound it

○ Feel your feet on the ground and your spine aligned

○ Close your eyes

○ Notice any sensations in your body and take a moment to allow it to relax

○ Bring your attention to the energy surrounding your body and feel for balance in it

○ Take a big breath in and as you sigh your breath out, let go of anything that gets in the way of you expressing your signature vibe. Next time you breathe in, imagine breathing in love and again sighing out anything that stops you expressing your signature vibe. Repeat this a few times

○ Take a deep breath down into your belly, connecting your head, heart and gut brains as you connect yourself up. Imagine as you take these deep breaths that you are bathing your cells in the love energy you have been breathing in

○ Take another of these long conscious breaths down into your belly as you slow down and become calmer

○ From the centre point in your chest, start to imagine a line going up through your body and all the way to the centre of the radiant sun

○ Now come back down the line into your body and down to the earth, all the way to the earth's molten core, feeling grounded

○ Feel aligned between the sun and the earth

○ Sense the energy in your heart centre starting to open and expand into your body

○ Allow this energy to expand beyond your body, merging with the energy around you, getting bigger and bigger

○ Expand that vibrant energy way out to encompass the whole earth, out past the planets and connecting to the infinite universe

- Expand out as far as you can possibly imagine, to where you have no edges and are fully connected to everything
- Notice and observe how it feels to be in your expanded energy field
- From that expanded place we can tune into everything and sense the energy within us and around us
- We all have our own personal vibrational frequency that we take out into the world. We are now going to get in touch with that frequency
- Call upon your awareness to tune into your vibrational frequency and allow you to express it. Just trust yourself and trust whatever happens
- Start to play with this. Hum your frequency and feel it vibrate on your lips. Try this a few times
- As you get used to the humming, extend it into sound by opening your mouth and throat and letting out whatever sound is there. Allow the sound, don't force it. It should be as if you are merely providing a channel for a sound that is already there. Keep playing with this; do it a few times until you find a sound that seems effortless to make and gives you the sense of coming home. A sign that you have found it is that it seems that you can sound it for an abnormally long period of time without needing to take a breath
- Really enjoy the experience of your personal vibe and notice your inner smile
- Open your eyes gently and start to take a few steps, embodying your signature vibe, realizing that you are not just a body, but also a field of energy that has a direct effect on the world around you
- If at first you feel that your personal frequency is at quite a low vibe, continue with the letting go exercises in Chapter 4 until you get to the acceptance frequency, as this opens up the possibility of raising your frequency to a higher vibration

HOW CAN YOU DEVELOP YOUR RELATIONSHIP WITH THE 'REAL YOU'?

Now that you have used your knowing to get an understanding of the real you, you can continue to expand your awareness of the real you into your whole being. This can be achieved by getting in touch with the energy that you have inside and starting to encourage it to flow through you.

Everything in the universe is energy, and we are a part of this universal energy field. We also have an inner energy that is referred to as chi, or life-force energy. This inner energy flows up the channel that goes from the base of your spine, the seat of your sexual energy, up to the crown of your head, connecting all of your energy centres.

It's an invisible, vital force that gives us life and weaves through all of creation. It can be the source of unlocking your potential, genius and creative powers, and accessing your true self. To access this energy, you need to be open and receptive. In order for the energy to be able to flow, the channel connecting your energy centres needs to be cleared of blocked emotions. When you close your energy centres and block your inner channel, you can't access this energy; when you open them you can.

When this energy is flowing, it fills you from the inside – you feel as though you can take on the world. It is what you feel when love rushes into your heart or when you are inspired. It is part of connecting to all of who you are. It is equally available to every-body, and it's unlimited. When it is flowing strongly, you can feel it coursing through you – restoring, replenishing and recharging you.

How will your life be enhanced when your life-force energy is flowing?

- It clears emotional blocks and may reveal blocked emotions so that you can let go of them
- You experience the best you: resilient, powerful, authentic and full

- It is cleansing and healing
- It increases your vibration
- It amplifies human experience
- You can experience more pleasure
- You can connect to bliss, purpose and joy
- You feel animated, alive and vibrant
- Your creativity and new ideas flow
- You can experience deeper love
- Synchronicities occur in your life and you are better connected with your true self
- You realize more potential, more genius

HOW OPEN ARE YOU TO A RELATIONSHIP WITH THE 'REAL YOU'?

The energy centre you intuitively know the most about opening and closing is your heart. In the presence of the ones you love, you feel very open because you trust them. So, you feel lots of high-frequency energy. But if they do something you don't like, the next time you see them you don't feel the high-frequency energy. You don't feel as much love. Instead you feel tightness in your chest. This happens because you have closed your heart. If they apologize to your satisfaction your heart may open again, and you may get filled with energy as love starts flowing again. You also do this in your relationship with yourself. You judge yourself, and even sometimes punish yourself subconsciously by blaming yourself (or others) instead of accepting and trusting life. Part of loving and caring for yourself is connecting with your life-force energy and expanding your experience of your true self.

Exercise 9 guides you to connect with your life-force energy.

Exercise 9
Connecting with your life-force energy

- Set an intention to expand to full connection and connect with your life-force energy, the energy that is the essence of who you really are
- Feel your feet on the ground and your spine aligned
- Close your eyes
- Notice any sensations in your body and take a moment to allow it to relax
- Bring your attention to the energy surrounding your body and feel for balance in it
- Take a deep breath in and as you sigh your breath out, let go of anything that is blocking the inner channel that connects your energy centres and through which your life-force energy flows. Keep sighing out anything blocking this channel
- Next time you breathe in, imagine breathing in love and again sigh out anything that stops your life-force energy from flowing. Repeat this a few times
- Take a deep breath down into your belly, connecting all of the energy centres making up your inner channel. Imagine as you keep taking these deep conscious breaths that your breath is continuing to clear that inner channel so that your life-force energy can flow through it
- Take another of these long conscious breaths down into your belly as you slow down and become calmer
- From the centre point in your chest, start to imagine a line going up through your body and all the way to the centre of the radiant sun, connect to the energy of the sun and the stars. Imagine bringing this beautiful bright life-force energy down the line and breathe it in through the crown of your head
- Now come back down the line into your body down through your inner channel right through the core of your body and down to the earth, all the way to the earth's molten core, feeling grounded
- Imagine how much life-force energy is held within the depths of the earth and visualize this energy. Now imagine you have nostrils under your feet and give yourself permission to breathe the earth's energy

upwards into your body through your feet. Notice how the swirling energy moves around your feet, causing them to tingle in anticipation of its journey into your body

○ Breathe in the universal life-force energy from the centre of the earth up through your feet into your body, up the channel through the core of your body that is parallel to your spine and which connects all of your energy centres. Keep breathing it up through your inner channel to the crown of your head. Do this twice more

○ Now start to circulate this energy by breathing it up through your pelvic floor, through your belly, solar plexus, heart, throat, behind your eyes and to the crown of your head. Then breath it out of the crown of your head and back down to your solar plexus. Keep circulating this life-force energy, raising its vibration as you do so. As you raise its vibration, you may start to see it as white light. Keep circulating it from your pelvic floor to the crown of your head a few more times

○ Now take your awareness to your personal source of life-force energy at the base of your spine. Allow yourself to tune into and connect with this energy made of love and light. Notice how it feels to be connecting with who you really are. Move this energy again up the inner channel through the core of your body until it arrives at your heart centre and start to allow this energy to expand outward beyond your body; as it expands it merges with the life-force energy around you getting bigger and bigger

○ Expand that vibrant life-force energy way out to encompass the whole earth, out past the planets and connecting to the infinite universe

○ Expand out as far as you can possibly imagine, to where you have no edges and are fully connected to everything

○ Notice and observe how it feels to be connected to your inner life-force energy, who you really are on the inside, and at the same time connected to the life-force energy in the energy field around you, being at one with this unified field of love and light

○ Open your eyes gently and know that this is the real you. You have the possibility to live your life from this place each and every day, with all the amazing potential that brings for you and those you connect with

WELLBEING - CARING FOR YOURSELF

There are other aspects of caring for yourself that encompass mental and physical wellness.

Mental health is a big issue in the UK, with many people suffering from some form of stress, anxiety or depression. Two thirds of British adults have experienced a mental health problem such as anxiety or depression, with less than a fifth experiencing high levels of positive mental health. Young people emerged as being most likely to suffer, with 70% of 18- to 34-year-olds saying they had experienced such problems, although middle-aged people (35–54) were close behind at 68%. The figure stood at 58% among those over the age of 55 (see Mental Health Foundation, *Fundamental Facts About Mental Health 2016*).

There is a spectrum of mental wellbeing and health that is influenced by many factors – your life situation, your body chemistry, your hormones. Looking at this at an energetic level reveals an energy imbalance. This imbalance is created when you suppress rather than express your emotions, thus creating blocked emotions in your system. These blocked emotions are usually unexpressed anger or sadness, which over time can lead to physical or mental disease.

All emotions have a vibrational frequency (see Chapter 2). When you feel anger toward someone, this feeling creates a sense of separation, which can be very damaging and leads to depression (situated at the bottom of the emotional frequency scale). This is the opposite of the connection felt from expressing love, a high-frequency emotion.

As discussed in Chapter 4 you can open yourself up by rewiring your limiting beliefs, interrupting your automatic patterns and clearing blocked emotions. Choosing to accept rather than suppress negative emotions, we can shift our energetic vibration, creating positive chemicals in the brain and the opportunity to transform and allow life to flow. Later, in Chapter 9, we will see that a natural part of going through transformation is to feel shock, denial, anger and sadness at the start of the transformational journey. Some people try to avoid the discomfort that accompanies strong negative emotions. Rather than seeing this as energy that needs to pass through, and a natural part of the ups and downs of life, they try to suppress them and sometimes label them as depression.

Energy imbalance can also affect our physical wellbeing. Our mental and physical wellbeing is intertwined at a cellular level. The low vibration of negative emotions creates cortisol and adrenaline in the body, which cells see as a threat, and they close themselves so as not to be contaminated. This means that at a cellular level we are not able to function at our best and ultimately the dis-ease in the cells causes physical disease. On the other hand, high vibrating positive emotions produce beneficial chemicals such as serotonin and dopamine, enabling us to access a state of flow and more of our potential. Many athletes have a practice that enables their bodies to function optimally and use positive sports psychology to get into a state of flow for peak performance.

Our sexual wellbeing is a key aspect of our physical wellbeing. As we will discover in Chapter 6, sexual energy is a force for us to use positively in our life.

The impact of nourishing the real you

By seeing yourself for who you really are and bringing your authentic self to all situations in your life, you will realize more of your potential and live a happier, more fulfilled life.

Seeing yourself for who you really are is the first step that prepares you to be able to see others for who they really are and have a profound effect on their lives too.

When you know you are loveable, you are attractive in the highest sense and your inner beauty shines out. The Law of

Attraction is not just about thinking positive thoughts; it starts with how you see yourself. You attract what you identify with. Therefore, if you feel loveable, you attract loving relationships because that's what you relate to. Loving yourself is the first step in creating a loving relationship. Other people become a reflection of the loving, kindly, peaceful relationship you have with yourself.

In short
KEY CONCEPTS FOR NOURISHING
THE REAL YOU

- Accepting yourself enables you to feel relaxed and enjoy who you are, which also determines the quality of your relationship with others
- When you feel disconnected, there is a gap between who you see yourself to be and who you really are
- Regular use of the Connection Practice, Exercise 7 (page 128) enables you to get familiar with your inner self and who you really are
- We all vibrate at a unique personal vibrational frequency or signature vibe; this is who we really are and others can pick up on this. Use Exercise 8 (page 130) to experience this or listen to the audio
- Caring for yourself is looking after your mental and physical wellbeing, and this involves connecting with your inner life force energy to understand yourself better. Use Exercise 9 (page 134) to do it
- By seeing your true self and being authentic, you will realize more of your potential and live a happier, more fulfilled life

HOW TO NOURISH THE REAL YOU
DAY TO DAY

- Every morning, imagine that you have made a new friend. Feel the love and support of your new friend. Now become that friend. Act toward yourself the way that friend would act toward you
- Take time each evening before going to sleep to write down three things that you are grateful for
- Do one thing each week that you are passionate about
- Cultivate your gifts and skills by taking up activities that make you feel good and connect you with people who make you feel good

Try it out for yourself! What are the first steps you intend to take to nourish the real you? Write them down.

Your Reflections

CHAPTER 6

Nurturing
Real-ationships

"If I accept the fact that my relationships are here to make me
conscious, instead of happy, then my relationships become
a wonderful self-mastery tool that keeps realigning me
with my higher purpose for living."

Eckhart Tolle

Core Beliefs: I accept others as they are and I see the potential in everyone.

Maybe you find yourself judging others. Perhaps you focus on what is not working and what is wrong in relationships rather than what is right. Possibly you believe others need fixing and aren't good enough. How can you move from this place of disconnection to one where you see others in their full potential and you are able to create true intimacy? Do you long for intimacy, but as soon as you get too close to someone you pull away?

In this chapter you will begin to understand how to create fully connected relationships, build true intimacy and so realize more of your relationship potential.

There are exercises in this chapter to support you in putting what you learn into practice. The best way to experience them is by being guided by us using the audio versions, which you can download using the link or QR code shared. Alternatively, you can do them by recording them on your phone and playing them back or by using the explanation in the text.

In the 21st century Western world, we talk about being hyper-connected, but what does that mean for our relationships? What we see is that we live in a mobile society full of temporary, superficial relationships. We are so busy that we have thin conversations. We communicate on the run using mobile phones and email. As a result, people are feeling a lack of human connection and are yearning for a greater sense of community. Our lives are so busy that we become very task focused, especially at work, where we are constantly asked to do more with less. But as social animals, we need connection. So how do we redress the balance and build real connection and intimacy in our lives? Before we start to address this, we need to know what we are working toward. What does an ideal relationship look like?

An ideal relationship is one that is real rather than superficial, and sustainable rather than temporary. It is a relationship where each party wants the best for the other party and so wants them to be able to be authentic, happy and realize their potential in life. It is a relationship between equals who recognize that they are a mirror for each other. Let's refer to these relationships as real-ationships.

There are four steps to having real-ationships:

1. Being real and authentic
2. Seeing others for who they really are
3. Developing real-ationship awareness
4. Growing in the real-ationship

Step 1: Being real and authentic

It is your state of being that enables you to develop real-ationships. You are present, expanded and connected. You can use the Connection Practice to maintain this state. Creating real-ationships requires us to open our hearts and be willing to be vulnerable. In our key relationships, it is about slowing down and creating the time and space to connect more deeply again and to be available for intimacy.

What do we mean by intimacy? It can be referred to as 'into-me-see'. It means allowing another person to see who you really are, being completely authentic and accepting the other for who they really are without wanting to change them.

Many people are afraid of intimacy and making themselves vulnerable. Have you ever been in a relationship with someone like this? What happens is that you put up walls around yourself. The walls go up because there's constant mind-talk trying to convince you that you are not enough and that you don't deserve to have a true connection. But you don't have to believe this.

Brené Brown says that sometimes we move away from things we need and crave the most, because we are afraid. So, if it is connection and intimacy that you run from, it is love you crave the most. When you realize that the only real need that human beings have is the need to connect, you can begin to act on it. You become aware that what causes disconnection is a gap between the self of your mind-talk and your real self. Use what you learned in the last chapter about seeing yourself as the real you, to get beyond the mind-talk and to be open to love and willing to be vulnerable.

Step 2: Other awareness

The next aspect of creating a real-ationship is how you see the other person in the relationship. Your job is to see their true self, someone with an amazing contribution to make, an equal presence of love. Honouring differences and seeing each other for who we really are helps us to grow into our real selves because we now know that how we see people is how they show up.

Neuroscience has shown us that our brains are equipped to naturally have empathy and build rapport. Our mirror neurons enable us to pick up subtle emotional cues and the feelings of others without even being conscious we are doing it. The information from the mirror neurons is processed very quickly. If we are aware enough to notice it, we can pick up on the feelings of the other person and choose how to behave in response. This ability creates resonance with others. In other words, it enables us to be on the same wavelength as others.

The feedback from mirror neurons is a two-way process. The impact of this is that we are constantly influencing each other's mood, judgments and behaviours. It means that our emotions are literally contagious. The person with the strongest emotional state can shift the emotional state of another person in two minutes – that's how powerful this ability is.

Your emotional state influences at an unconscious level how people feel about you. It determines whether people are open or closed to you. It determines whether you are able to build empathy and rapport with someone. It also influences whether they are in a positive, open emotional state, which affects their ability to perform at their best and think clearly.

What implications does this have for your relationships? You can develop an awareness of an emotional state and the ability to manage it so that it has a positive impact on others. You can also develop your ability to tune into the emotional state of others and show empathy and connect with them. We all have these abilities naturally through our mirror neurons, but many of us choose not to use them.

You can use the Connection Practice to expand to a pure being place. You can use your knowing to connect with the pure being place in the other person. When you appreciate the real self of another person, you see that person in the light of your real self. That is real love – you see your real self in the mirror of the real-ationship.

Hindus and Buddhists use a beautiful way of greeting another person called Namaste, which is based on this notion of how you see others is how they will show up.

In Sanskrit, 'Namaste', pronounced Na-ma-stay, means 'the divine in me bows to the divine to you'. Namaste is a greeting that shows that you are honouring the other person as a mirror of yourself. When we are able to see another human being as a mirror, both comfortable and uncomfortable meetings can ultimately become gifts. Namaste is about looking more deeply than the level of personality and connecting with the essential humanness of the other person, the level at which we are all equal and all the same. You can greet yourself with a Namaste in the mirror and you can use it with your partner, friends and relatives. By performing Namaste, you show deep respect to others.

In Exercise 10 we share with you the steps to doing a simple Namaste with another person.

Exercise 10
How you see others is how
they will show up – Namaste

- Begin by sitting or standing opposite your partner or your own reflection in the mirror. Come into eye contact in silence. Let your arms hang loose and relaxed
- Press your palms together in a prayer position in front of your chest. Your wrists should be centred on your ribcage and not below
- Point your fingers upward. Hold your fingers together rather than spreading them apart as you touch your hands together. Your thumbs should be pressed firmly against your body, so there is no gap between your chest and your hands
- Bow slightly. With a straight back, bend forward from the hips and, keeping your eyes open, let your forehead touch that of the other person or just let your eyes connect. Pause for one second at the lowest point of the bow
- Still holding your hands in place, move back up-right to a straightened posture. Acknowledge any gratitude you feel for this meeting as your focus returns to your heart
- Say "Namaste". Keeping your eyes connected with the other person, both say Namaste. Namaste is often said in a calm and peaceful voice. It is a bit like a blessing, recognizing the divine in the person you are greeting

You are now ready to interact with the person you're greeting.

Step 3: Real-ationship awareness

Life is made up of relationships consisting of all the people we feel connected to. When you say "I relate to x," no matter who x is, you have made a connection. When you do not relate to someone, the opposite has occurred. You feel disconnected.

So, any time you interact with another person, there will be a successful connection or a failure to connect. But if we want to truly master the art of real-ationships, we need to develop our awareness of when we are connecting and when we are disconnecting.

When you disconnect, you switch off and close down so that your attention and love no longer flow outward; you retreat into yourself or shield yourself with defence mechanisms. These are some of the defence mechanisms people experience when they are disconnected and only in their heads:

- Distracted and unable to be present
- Repetitive thinking influenced by past experiences
- Often negative fear-based thoughts
- Stuck thoughts lacking in solutions
- Narrow focus, unable to see the bigger picture
- Caught up in the drama and story
- Obsessive thinking
- Judgmental, blaming and critical
- Taking everything personally and magnifying them
- Playing the victim, 'poor me'
- Taking offence
- Attacking
- Wanting to be right – ego
- Rigidity
- Denial
- Withdrawal into silence
- Confusion
- Addiction: alcohol, drugs, shopping, food, screens, etc.

Maybe you have experienced some of these in yourself and others. Coming out of disconnection requires us to stop blaming others and believing that they made us disconnect through their negative behaviour and/or to stop judging and blaming ourselves by assuming we did something to cause the disconnect. By using the Connection Practice to get into a centred, expanded state, you can learn to control the on/off switch of connection. From this place, you can see what's really going on and see that you have the ability to change any situation by seeing it for what it really is and the potential it offers. This is where you both see the opportunity to grow and create win-win situations.

Sue had a distant relationship with her mother after her childhood. However, a silver lining of her cancer diagnosis was that her mother came to look after her following each chemotherapy session. They took the opportunity of this time together to connect at a deep level and as a result their relationship transformed into a positive, loving real-ationship.

What makes relationships challenging often comes down to one factor – we build the relationship from the outside in, believing something we want is not happening because of someone else who is outside of us.

Real-ationships are created from the inside out. Even though it takes two people to build the real-ationship, the responsibility for connecting starts with you. Real-ationships are never automatic: they need attention. As you use the Connection Practice to have more awareness of when you are connected and when you are disconnecting, you will turn relationships around in every area of life because you will know how to keep connections alive.

All the relationships in your life have a purpose and once that purpose is realized the relationship may end or evolve to find a new purpose. There is an opportunity in all relationships to find the gift of learning and growth they are bringing. In most relationships, this will only happen if you are self-aware and have a growth mindset. That way you will notice the challenge in the relationship and be open to explore what is being reflected back to you in terms of your growth and opening up. The other person in the relationship is responsible for their growth and may or may not choose to do something about it. In real-ationships, there is a conscious decision to support each other's growth so that each individual and the relationship itself realizes their potential. You might want to explore the state of your real-ationship on the three following levels.

1. Sensing for balance in the real-ationship

Does giving feel balanced by receiving? If not, what is causing the imbalance?

The back and forth in a relationship can run into problems for a number of reasons, such as one or both people may have stopped communicating well. What's important is not the reason but the feeling of disconnect.

The disconnect might be as a result of a lack of alignment in how you express love. Don't assume that what works for you when expressing love works for the other person (see Gary Chapman, *The 5 Love Languages*).

2. Knowing when you are connecting and when you aren't

Trust is the foundation of every relationship and can be experienced on many different levels. What's the level of trust in your relationship? Long before a relationship reaches the point where two people are tuning each other out, a subtler disconnect has occurred. This is a break in trust – a process that must be kept alive. Think of this as a trust bank account. Ask yourself, "Is this bank account healthy or is it in the red?" Eventually, if the account becomes too overdrawn, the relationship becomes disconnected and ultimately it may reach a point of no return.

3. Assessing the level of dependency
versus interdependency

Tune into your relationship and get a sense of how safe you feel. How safe is it to be your real self? When you connect at the level of the real self, you remain centred and safe. On the one hand, you are connected intimately with another, and on the other hand you are still in full possession of your own awareness. This is the state of interdependency, which allows you to have intimacy without being lost or suffocated by it.

Step 4: Growing in the real-ationship

Not all of the relationships in your life will be real-ationships. However, all relationships offer the potential for growth if you are self-aware enough and open to learning and growing. It is especially the relationships you find most difficult, that trigger you and surface your stuff, that offer this potential. The personal growth from these relationships is your responsibility and you are not responsible for whether or not the other person grows. That depends on their openness and readiness to grow.

A real-ationship is dynamic. It's an opportunity for *mutual* growth. We usually only have a few real-ationships at any one time in our lives. Real-ationships are the ones in which there is a conscious willingness to learn from each other and challenge each other with the intention of supporting growth. In this sort of relationship, there is space for each individual to grow as well as for the co-created relationship to grow.

Reflect on a real-ationship in your life, which probably means a partner or spouse, parent, sibling, your own adult child or a best friend. Look at the one that feels the most positive to you, where you turn for real connection. How is the real-ationship supporting growth for both of you?

What makes a real-ationship positive is a steady process that keeps you both growing and feeling alive inside. If you are going to share your evolution with someone else, you both have to be comfortable with closeness – not necessarily physical intimacy, but open from heart to heart. Your discomfort and your emotions are your responsibility, but at any time you can count on the other person to be empathetic and nonjudgmental. Boundaries exist to be stretched but not intentionally violated. At their best, real-ationships bring people together in full connection and can be the source of the greatest joy.

> "If we have no peace it is because we have
> forgotten that we belong to each other."
> ## Mother Teresa

Keeping the connection alive is a challenge. The first thing is to make a commitment to see each other for who we really are, no matter what arises. You are choosing to relate from love, not fear. Consciously choosing to stay connected in this way will bring you unlimited potential for growth in terms of peace, love, intimacy, honesty, sharing, compassion and moving together on a shared journey with your partner.

Robert had a big wake-up call when he was going through a divorce. He was feeling angry, fearful and anxious, having panic attacks and feeling revengeful. The Connection Practice helped him get his bitterness and resentment out so he could come back to himself and connect from there rather than from a codependent place. First, he dealt with his relationship with himself. He started to look after himself, including his nutrition and physical fitness. He also started doing things he enjoyed. From there he was able to look at his relationships, especially with his daughter and new girlfriend, and find a more authentic way of being in them. As his true self started to shine through, he was able to relax and be present, sharing his love in an authentic way. His relationship with his children has gone from strength to strength and he is in love again with a beautiful woman. He now uses the Connection Practice to expand into what he calls his whole self and into a state of love.

USING THE CONNECTION PRACTICE FOR SEEING WHO PEOPLE REALLY ARE AND SEEING THEIR POTENTIAL

Being able to see those with whom you have relationships for who they really are will not only support them in realizing their own potential but will support you both in realizing the potential in the relationship.

Exercise 11
Seeing who people really are

Find someone to do this with or just imagine the person you want to work with being with you:

o Connect with the love for yourself

o Breathe in and out and connect to your true self, your love and compassion for yourself, accepting your uniqueness and perfection. Feel the love for yourself so you then know how to love another

o Allow yourself to access that place in yourself that is nonjudgmental and unconditional and set an intention to use your knowing to connect with the full potential of the person opposite you and see them for who they really are

o Feel your feet on the ground and your spine aligned

o Close your eyes

o Notice any sensations in your body and take a moment to allow it to relax

o Bring your attention to the energy surrounding your body and feel for balance in it

o Take a big breath in and as you sigh your breath out, let go of anything that gets in the way of connecting with the potential of this other person. Repeat this a few times

○ Take a deep breath down into your belly, connecting your head, heart and gut brains as you connect yourself up

○ Take another of these long conscious breaths down into your belly as you slow down and become calmer

○ From the centre point in your chest, start to imagine a line going up through your body and all the way to the centre of the radiant sun

○ Now come back down the line into your body and down to the earth, all the way to the earth's molten core, your source energy, feeling grounded

○ Feel aligned between the sun and the earth

○ Sense the energy of love in your heart centre starting to open. See this energy expand into your body

○ Allow this energy to expand beyond your body, merging with the energy around you, getting bigger and bigger

○ Expand that vibrant energy way out to encompass the whole earth, out past the planets and connecting to the infinite universe

○ Expand out as far as you can possibly imagine, to where you have no edges and are fully connected to everything

○ From this expanded state, tune into the person sitting opposite you/ imagine that another person is sitting opposite you. Imagine that you are connected by a field of unconditional love. Imagine this is the most extraordinary being you've ever come across, who's been in disguise up until now

○ Now imagine that you are tuning into that amazing being as you would tune into the frequency of a radio station. Once you are tuned in, ask him/her to reveal who they really are, what the contribution is that they are here to make. Your job is to imagine them into their magnificence. Ask to see who they really are and let the pictures, feelings, symbols, sensations, colours just come to you to give you clues as to who this person really is and what their contribution/potential is

○ Allow the answers to come into your knowing. Be patient and trust without judgment whatever comes

○ Now open your eyes. Really tune into what you saw and feed it back to the other person in the most empowering way possible

- Swap, or if you are imagining the person, take your journal and write them a letter telling them what you saw. You can choose to send this letter or not as feels appropriate
- When you appreciate the real self of another person, you see that person in the light of your real self. That is real love — you see your real self in the mirror of the real-ationship

Exercise 11 is great to do energetically before meeting someone on either a personal or professional level. If a disconnect occurs between you and your partner, you can use the Connection Practice to get into an expanded state. This will enable you to see what is really happening and then speak what needs to be spoken or truly listen to co-create the way forward.

Seeing others for who they really are enables you to create an attitude of unconditional love and acceptance in which they can shine and bring more of themselves. It starts with you bringing all of yourself, with a capacity for self-love and then creating that state in yourself so that you can connect fully with others. The Connection Practice helps you to access that state of inner peace and calm where everything is just love.

FULL CONNECTION SEXUAL WELLBEING AND INTIMACY

We mentioned that sexual wellbeing is an important aspect of overall wellbeing in the last chapter. It is an important part of life for many people.

Even in the 21st century this subject is still a bit taboo, or at least an embarrassing subject for some people. The reason some people still find it difficult to be open about their sex life is that there is often a performance pressure and/or body image anxiety related to it. This can cause them to disconnect.

How does being disconnected affect your sex life? You are closed down, your senses are dulled, you are not feeling your emotions, and are judgmental and critical. As a result, you don't feel an emotional connection to your partner. You may feel that you have to look or perform in a certain way, which is not authentic to how you are really feeling and what you are really wanting.

What is the effect of being fully connected in your sex life? You are fully present in the moment, your senses are heightened, your heart is fully open, so you feel a deeper connection with and love for your partner. You can experience more pleasure and there is a mutual desire to give and receive pleasure. There is an opportunity to create an enhanced shared experience by unifying and expanding both your energies and bringing them into coherence and a sense of being one. Who would not want to experience the bliss, ecstasy and joy that this has the potential to ignite?

Physical and emotional intimacy are profound human experiences of sharing, but when we connect true self to true self, we can experience a love that goes beyond personal pleasure or affection and find the freedom to be our true unbounded self.

What we are talking about here is a practical way of using energy to enhance your health, wellbeing and sexual fulfilment. The alchemical effect of the positive emotions and chemicals in the body, as well as the raising of your vibrational frequency, can have a profound effect on your physical, emotional and mental wellbeing. This is part of experiencing the real you and bringing her/him out to play!

Did anybody ever explain to you how your sexual energy works? Although the male body and the female body are similar, they are also complementary opposites. The attraction exists because male and female are half-circuits, and as in an electrical circuit, when the positive connects to the negative and the negative connects to the positive, they unite in a circle of electrical energy with a moment of unity and completion.

Everyone falls somewhere on the spectrum of gender from female to male; we are each a blend of female and male in varying proportions. Yin (female) and yang (male), dynamic and receptive, positive and negative, the integration of these polarities mean that when people are in sexual union, the bio-energies of their bodies, their life-force, create an ecstatic state or sexual experience.

Our personal source of life-force energy is located at the base of our spine. Within sexual union, this energy starts to flow up through our energy centres, through the energy channels (meridians) in the body, and fills our body with an increase of energy at a cellular level. In this way, we are able to heal ourselves of any energy imbalance as our bodies gradually return to their male and female polarities, healing us in the process from many of our problems, anxieties and illnesses. This is a major energy source. Most people don't know how to harness and use the power of their sexual energy; they leak it out unconsciously and it leaves them feeling energetically depleted. How can we amplify the pleasure and power it gives us? The life-force energy that is the essence of sexual connection builds and peaks at the time of orgasm. The key to this is expanding and recirculating your energy throughout the sexual encounter. In doing so, you expand the flow of sexual energy and the experience of orgasm to a full-body orgasm.

As the life-force energy moves up through the energy centres, more energy reaches the higher centres, thus allowing us to experience a feeling of expansion and connection to the whole field of energy from which we came. This expansive feeling is heightened because the body transforms itself into a kind of instrument or tuning device that raises our vibration as the energy spirals upward, bringing with it bliss and ecstasy.

By channelling your sexual energy in this way, you feel vibrant and happy. This feeling spreads into all that you do and you can experience a sense of flow for hours or even days afterwards. It is as if you are tuned into the rhythms of life.

The experience of becoming one by connecting your life-force energy with that of your partner

We have created a bonus exercise in which we guide you to use a breathing technique helping you to create a shared flow of life-force energy between you and your partner, creating a feeling of being one. It is available to download using the link below or scanning the QR code:

thezoneofconnection.com/bonuses

In short
KEY CONCEPTS FOR NURTURING
REAL-ATIONSHIPS IN YOUR DAILY LIFE

- All relationships have a purpose, and when that purpose is realized the relationships may end or evolve and find a new purpose
- A real-ationship is between equals who recognize that they are a mirror for each other and want the best for each other. They are created from the inside out
- Four keys to developing real-ationships – being real and authentic, relating from love not fear, being aware of when you are disconnected, growing in the relationship
- To connect more deeply and be available for intimacy, you need to slow down and see others for who they really are. Use Exercise 11 (page 153) and connect from your true self to the true self of others

HOW TO NURTURE REAL-ATIONSHIPS
DAY TO DAY

- Daily practice of gratitude – think of all people in your life that you feel grateful for having and why
- Practice seeing people for who they really are, even in difficult situations. Consciously do this before having conversations, do it energetically before meeting people, do it with your children and close family. Don't tell others what to do, but trust that they have the resources to find their own solutions and ways of doing things

Try it out for yourself! What are the first steps you intend to take to nurture real-ationships in your life? Write them down.

Your Reflections

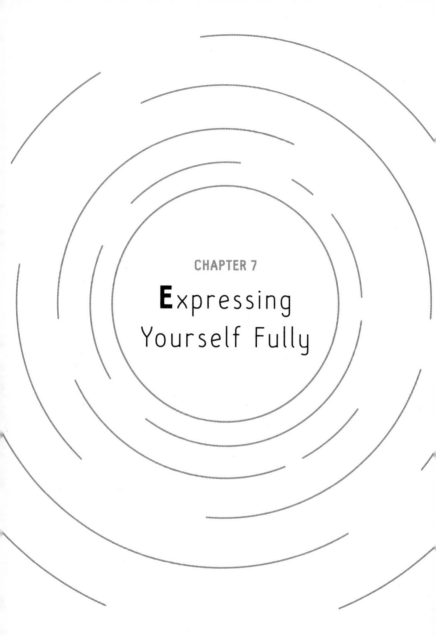

CHAPTER 7

Expressing Yourself Fully

"If you just communicate you can get by, but if you communicate skilfully you can create miracles!"
Jim Rohn

Core Belief: I trust my intuition, knowing and wisdom.

One evening Penny found herself sitting next to a general at a dinner. Her heart sank and her energy dropped as she sat down and wondered what on earth she was going to have in common with him. Then she realized that she had judged this man and put him in a box based on loaded limiting beliefs. In that moment, she knew that she had a choice and decided to imagine that he was the most interesting person she had ever met! By using the Connection Practice, she was able to communicate with him in a way that transformed her experience and he truly became a very interesting person and she had a wonderful, fun evening.

In this chapter, we will get a clear understanding of what communicating fully offers and experience for ourselves how to do it. As human beings, we cannot not communicate! Communication is so much more than words. We are energy beings and can powerfully communicate on many levels, including through body language and the energetic vibration we send out. With this understanding, we can power up our communication to the level of full communication where we are fully connected to others and ourselves. Communicating in this way we co-create a safe, creative space in which together we transcend personal communication, allowing a collective knowing to come through and so accessing full communication.

WHAT IS FULL COMMUNICATION?

Communication is a multilayered phenomenon. It exists on multiple levels, which are all intertwined and dance together, conveying messages through words, nonverbal/body language and energy signals. The more people involved in the communication, the more complex and multilayered it becomes.

When developing his Communication Model, Professor Albert Mehrabian discovered that words only represent 7% of what we communicate. Tone of voice is 38% and body language 55%. Communication is therefore an experience far richer than words alone can convey. It is not as dependent on words as we may imagine, yet they have an important role to play. Words are like signposts directing you toward a fuller understanding, which we believe can only be reached if we are open and in a connected state.

Full communication is about being in an open state where you can receive and give information and not become reactive or take things personally. Instead you welcome the communication and are open to understand and appreciate its meaning. There may have been times when you have wanted to say something but held yourself back and were not able to say what you really mean. With full communication, when you speak, you are able to express yourself and your truth from a place of nonjudgment and potential, saying what is there to be spoken from your knowing. Until expressing what is true for us becomes natural.

Have you ever felt frustrated when you are talking about something that is important to you and the person you are speaking to is distracted and not really listening? When you truly listen, you are able to receive that knowing from a place of nonjudgment and potential. Your listening in this way transforms the communication. When we learn to communicate in a true way, we realize that listening is as important as speaking. This is because we now understand that everything is interrelated and that the listener actually co-creates what is said and expressed. Full communication includes your self-talk and how you talk to yourself, which has a profound effect on your life.

WHY DOES IT MATTER?

Full communication matters on three levels:

It affects the energy field: in which communication takes place by raising the frequency, which enhances feelings of safety and trust, encouraging authenticity and enabling full expression of the real you. The higher vibrational frequency creates feel-good chemicals in the brain and shifts the energy field to a transformational level.

It affects our relationships: being able to express ourselves fully from a place of nonjudgment is at the heart of a good relationship. Being able to communicate fully is one of the things that creates intimacy (into-me-see). This is what we all want to have and enjoy: our desire to have close, deep relationships. The skill of full communication is very helpful in conflict situations and with people we find difficult, giving us a more expansive perspective, compassion, and clearer understanding of others and ourselves. It takes people beyond their limitations and helps them access their whole being and potential – to be all that they can be.

It affects the impact we have: mastery of this extraordinary skill and using it in our daily life dramatically affects our impact. The impact we have starts with our conscious intention. The purpose of and intention behind full communication is to help others go beyond their limitations, fully express themselves, ignite their undiscovered potential and shine their light in the world.

Our energy emanates from us so without even saying a word, we have an impact on every single person that we meet. Our energy ripples out and can have either a positive or negative effect. If our state of being is open, loving and connected, we communicate that energy to others. If we are closed down, judgmental and disconnected, we communicate that too. Our personal vibrational frequency is what ripples out into the world around us and it is up to us to manage that frequency so that we have the impact we desire. We are a lot more influential than we sometimes realize!

THE SCIENTIFIC EXPLANATION
OF HOW IT WORKS

You'll remember how we explained that everything is made up of energy and it is there for us to sense and use as data input. What we think, our emotions and intentions, and what we perceive, affects the world around us. We are powerful energy beings and our potential to affect others is a great gift and a responsibility. Becoming aware of and taking responsibility for this energetic influence allows us to manage how we influence others. This is explained by the Law of Entrainment.

Law of Entrainment

Everything has a frequency. As we have seen in Chapter 2, love and gratitude are high-frequency energies, which we experience when we are connected, whereas fear and anger are low-frequency energies and a sign of disconnection.

Entrainment is when two or more different frequencies get to synchronize with each other. When two or more entities are vibrating at their individual frequencies, the one with the strongest frequency will have the others synchronize to it. If you have a room full of pendulum clocks and start them all swinging at different rhythms, they will synchronize with each other. The smaller pendulums entrain to the strongest vibration.

Have you ever been around someone or something that felt so negative that you felt drained and depleted? Your energy has entrained to their energy. You start vibrating to their frequency. What usually happens is that you avoid people or situations that you perceive as negative. This causes even more problems, as it shuts you down. Not only does this stop you from exuberantly radiating your light, but it also reduces your energy field so that you are more vulnerable to outside influences and attract more of what you are trying to avoid.

You can become the strongest energy in the room. If your positive energy is radiantly strong, other people will entrain to it. For us to be the strongest energy, we need to be in a state of energetic coherence, with our three brains working together. This is a state of full connection; you are connecting at all levels including head, heart, gut and whole being.

With full communication, you speak coherently from your whole being and energy field. This raises your frequency and through entrainment you raise the frequency of the other person you are communicating with. This in turn creates a safe space of trust and acceptance where you can both be authentic.

Neuroscience adds to this understanding by explaining how our mirror neurons work (see Chapter 2). These neurons help us tune into the emotions of others and also mean that we imitate others. So, if your energy is the strongest energy in the room, it is likely that others will not only entrain to it, but also imitate your behaviours.

Through neuroscience, we also understand that we all have a preference either for our frontal lobes (language centre) or our sensory lobes at the back of our brain. People who focus more electrochemical activity in the frontal lobes are expressive/extroverted and think through speaking. Those who focus more electrochemical activity in the back/the sensory lobes are reflective/introverted and more likely to be good at listening. They absorb information through the senses and prefer to process it internally before speaking. Full communication balances the use of the front and back of the brain, expanding the energetic impact of what is being said.

HOW DO WE MASTER
FULL COMMUNICATION?

Full communication involves mastering both full listening and speaking from a place of full connection, where you are present, expanded and open to infinite possibilities.

Full listening is well beyond active listening; it's a deeper level of listening. Once you are in a fully connected state by using the Connection Practice, you connect with each other true self to true self, seeing the other person in all of their potential. You both tune into your knowing and co-create what wants to be said. This will also result in the speaker being able to express themselves fully, speaking beyond the confines of their conscious mind. You will experience that listening is as important as speaking when you use full communication.

Full speaking enables us to powerfully express what we have connected to from our knowing. This is a creative process and a first step to manifesting desires by expressing them into the world. It is not about preparing or thinking, but surrendering into the moment and letting your knowing flow through you. There is a different tonal quality to full speaking and different words are likely to be used. When we speak from this deep level, the audience becomes fully engaged and they feel resonance with the speaker as their passion, brilliance and genius shines through. In turn, this raises everyone's vibration to a higher energy frequency, inspiring the audience to access their own brilliance and genius.

Speaking in this way, you astound yourself and can't quite believe what has been spoken through you or even remember what you said! The audience also has a feeling of amazement, not only at what has been said, but at the transformational effect it has had on them.

Here are some of the amazing benefits from using the Connection Practice to access full communication:

- You will be able to speak your truth and fully express yourself
- It will take your relationships to a conscious level and help you see beyond difficulties and conflict to potential
- It creates a safe space for intimacy (into-me-see) to unfold
- The co-creation of an expanded high-vibe energy field attracts even bigger possibilities to you
- It ensures everyone involved feels heard and acknowledged and experiences deeper connection

There are two exercises in this chapter to support you in putting what you learn into practice. The best way to experience them is by being guided by us using the audio versions which you can download using the link or QR code shared. Alternatively, you can do them by recording them on your phone and playing them back or by using the explanation in the text.

Exercise 12
Different levels of communication:
head, heart to whole being

This exercise involves communicating from the head, heart and gut; noticing how it feels; noticing the different sort of words you use at each level; and noticing the impact on the other person.

Ideally, you'll want to ask someone to do these exercises with you. If that is not possible, you can also just experiment by using the technique when you next speak and listen to someone.

Communicating from the head brain

You know what it feels like when you're speaking and you know the other person is not really listening? This happens when we listen using our head brain only.

Try this listening exercise out with someone:

o Focus hard on the thoughts in your head only and not on what you or the other person is saying

o Allow yourself to be distracted by your thoughts; you may think how boring this is or what am I going to have for supper tonight — there is not much listening going on

o Notice and observe what you feel, notice the sort of words you use and notice the impact on the other person

Speaking from the head, focusing on the energy in the head, results in bland talking. This is hard to listen to and can come across as nervousness, lack of confidence or being in story/drama mode. It is monotone and unexciting to listen to and causes those listening to tune out. It sounds a bit like 'blah blah blah' when they speak, and is boring and often problem oriented. When we think and act from mental intelligence alone, we are just talking heads: programs talking to programs. Try it for yourself and notice the impact it has on the person listening to you.

Communicating from the heart brain

Now try focusing only on the energy in your heart centre, where your heart brain is.

○ Tune in and place your attention there, place your hand on your heart, then allow your speech and listening to come from your heart
○ Notice and observe what you feel, notice the sort of words you used and notice the impact on the other person

Listening from your heart, you feel empathy with what the person is really trying to say. Speaking from the heart is where a person speaks from their passion with energy and excitement. The speaking comes from deep inside, saying what they really want to say, engaging others to be eager to listen.

Communication from the gut brain

○ Think of something that you might want an answer to
○ Close your eyes and place your hand and awareness just below your belly button
○ Ask the question and allow your gut brain to respond
○ Notice and observe what this feels like; be open and curious as to what comes to you

This is about communicating from your gut feel and the knowing that you have about something. You can also use this when you are speaking with someone and want to tune into what they are really saying or even what they are not saying.

Exercise 13
Full communication: communicating from the whole being

This is best done as a partner exercise, taking it in turns to listen and speak.

○ Set your intention to reach a state of full connection and to access full communication

○ Feel your feet on the ground and your spine aligned

○ Close your eyes

○ Notice any sensations in your body and take a moment to allow it to relax

○ Bring your attention to the energy surrounding your body and feel for balance in it

○ Take a big breath and let go of anything you don't need right here and now

○ Breathe in from your head, down through your heart to your gut, connecting yourself up

○ Take another long conscious, calming breath, slowing down

○ From the centre point in your chest, start to imagine that line going up through your body and all the way to the centre of the radiant sun

○ Now come back down the line into your body and down to the earth, all the way to the earth's molten core, your source energy, feeling grounded

○ Feel aligned between the sun and the earth

○ Sense the energy in your heart centre starting to open and expand into your body

○ Allow this energy to expand beyond your body, merging with the energy around you, getting bigger and bigger

○ Expand way out into that vibrant energy to encompass the whole earth, out past the planets and connecting to the infinite universe

○ As far as you can possibly imagine where you have no edges and are fully connected to everything

- Connect with your knowing about the potential of what wants to be spoken
- Feel your energy field in the space around you affecting everything in the world
- Now open your eyes and connect with your partner. Allow yourself to receive their gaze, keeping half of your awareness inside and notice the relational space; see your partner as a massive, whole, passionate being with unlimited potential
- From that place, speak authentically and listen with powerful attention and curiosity
- Speaker: tune into your biggest potential in the moment and into what wants to be said through you now, and let it flow through you
- Listener: truly listen, really leaning in with excitement about the potential of what the person is about to say. Feel your field of presence expand, letting the information land in the space. Now listen transformatively to who this person really is and what amazing things want to be said through them
- Thank your partner for doing this with you and take it in turns to share your experience — what did you notice, what was different, how do you feel, what did you learn?

Speaking to a group, or speaking publicly to an audience, can be an intimidating experience for some people. By being in the ZOC, in a state of full connection before you speak, you also reap all of the benefits, which include feeling relaxed, clear and excited rather than nervous and fearful! It enables you to powerfully express what you have connected to from your knowing so that the speaking comes from beyond yourself, opening infinite possibilities and awakens, stirs and touches people deeply. When you speak from this deep level, the audience becomes fully engaged and they feel resonance with the speaker as their passion, brilliance and genius shine through. This in turn raises everyone's vibration to a higher energy frequency, inspiring the audience to access their own brilliance and genius.

We have created a bonus exercise that supports you in doing this when speaking in front of a group. It is available to download using the link below or scanning the QR code:

thezoneofconnection.com/bonuses

In short
KEY CONCEPTS FOR
BETTER COMMUNICATION

- We are energy beings and powerfully communicate on many levels, including through body language and the energetic vibration we send out; it is a multilayered phenomenon
- We can improve the way we communicate to the level where we are fully connected to others and ourselves
- Full communication affects the energy field, our relationships and the impact we have through entrainment of our energetic frequency

HOW TO USE FULL COMMUNICATION
IN YOUR DAILY LIFE

- Try the full communication Exercise 13 (page 172) when you are listening to your family, children or partner and also in difficult or conflict situations. Remember, listening is as important as speaking
- After the Connection Practice, feel your field of presence expand so what is said can land in the space around you. Now see people for who they really are and listen to what amazing things are being said through them. Notice what effect this has
- If you feel that you have been thrown off balance, a quick way to bring yourself back is to place your hand on your heart and say to yourself: I love you and I'm listening

Try it out for yourself! What are the first steps you intend to take to integrate full communication into your daily life? Write them down.

Your Reflections

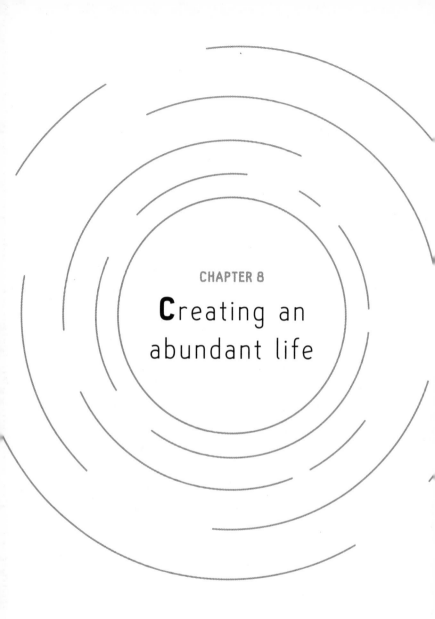

CHAPTER 8

Creating an abundant life

"Imagination is the beginning of creation.
You imagine what you desire, you will what you
imagine and at last you create what you will."
George Bernard Shaw

Core Belief: Life is abundant.

PENNY'S DREAM COME TRUE

I am walking by the sea in Dorset and take a moment to sit on a rock in the sun with my dog, Red, by my side. Out of the blue, the realization dawns on me that I have actually created the life I have been dreaming of! For a moment, I am paralysed with awe and then a wave of gratitude sweeps over me. For so long I have imagined being in a deeply loving relationship and sharing my life intimately, creating a beautiful home near the sea, where I can enjoy my wonderful family, friends and dog, feeling healthy and in balance and making a difference in people's lives and the world through my work. How amazing that I have created all of this!

There was a time when I felt that life was just happening to me. Maybe you feel this, or that you have no choice or say in what happens. Perhaps you fear that your life is off track and going in the wrong direction. It could be that you are resigned to the fact that your dreams will never be realized or that you can't see a clear vision for your future.

You're possibly thinking – so how do you change all of this? What if it were true that the magic of being a human being lies in our ability to create and manifest and that it is our birthright to lead an abundant life? This would mean that you are the master of your life and you have the power to choose and create the life you want.

The Law of Attraction is real and always at work, whether you choose to recognize and engage with it or not. You can learn to cultivate it and attract what you most want into your life and this is what we'll explore now.

IT ALL STARTS WITH VIBRATION AND ENERGY!

The Law of Attraction breaks down into a number of different components. The first is the Law of Vibration. The Law of Vibration states that everything that exists in our universe, whether visible or not, can be quantified as a frequency or an energy pattern. Everything, including us, has its own unique vibration or personal energy.

This unique vibration is created from the combination of your thoughts and intentions, feelings and emotions (see Chapter 2).

The Law of Attraction also states that 'Like attracts like'. What this means is that whatever frequency you are vibrating, you will attract into your life things at the same frequency. For example, if you choose happy feelings, more happy feelings will be drawn into vibrational harmony with them. If, on the other hand, you are constantly angry and fearful, then you will be creating more of the same in your life. You create your personal vibration and beam that frequency out into the world, and whatever your energy patterns are will come back to you in the form of things, people and experiences that match your vibration. So, the first step is to tune your vibration to the same frequency as what you want to attract.

We understand that our thoughts help create our vibration and therefore play a key part in creating our reality. Our thoughts do this by influencing our feelings and emotions. The energy of our emotions passes through our body and that charge gets pulsed out into the energy field and draws like energy to us. If you think something over and over again, it creates a stronger emotional charge and that charge will eventually attract a person or a circumstance into your life that matches that emotional vibration.

We know that a lot of our automatically programmed thinking is negative and problem related, and therefore attracts negativity. Our inner world is a perfect mirror of what we create in our outer world. If we still have deeply buried negative thoughts inside, we set up the Law of Paradoxical Intent, meaning that we attract more of those negative circumstances. Thinking positively is not enough if at the same time you are pushing negative emotions down deep inside you; feeling that you do not deserve abundance in your life, or fear that you will not get what you want, your energy is restricted. You want to be very aware of what you are thinking and, more importantly, the emotions you are feeling in your body in response to your thoughts, letting go of anything that does not serve you. One way to focus your thoughts is to consciously set intentions that are aligned with what you want.

You have the choice to learn to tune into your emotional frequency. Negative emotions vibrate at a low frequency, so that's what you are going to draw to you. Also, if you are thinking about what you don't want, you're actually experiencing feelings associated with what you don't want. As a result, you're going to keep attracting over and over again experiences and circumstances that reflect feelings of what you don't want. And we know you don't want to do that!

On the other hand, positive emotions vibrate at a higher frequency. So imagine what you want to create and get in touch with the feelings associated with it. You can choose to generate those feelings any time you want and shift to that vibrational frequency. The more you feel that emotion, the more that becomes your dominant vibration and becomes your reality. You start attracting more and more experiences into your life that mirror how you already feel. This is why it's so important that you pay attention to how you *feel*, not just what you think.

For example: you don't want more money just for the sake of it, because that in itself is empty; you want more freedom, you want more opportunities. You want that because you want to feel a certain way, and in knowing how you want to feel, you can clarify what you really want. Pay attention to why you want something, not just what you want.

Having love and abundance is your birthright. The key to attracting this is to trust that it will be so and to elevate your frequency in all areas of your life. If you do this, your positive energy is so radiantly strong you will feel empowered no matter who or what else is in your environment. As you raise your vibration, everything in your life gets better. Not only that, but your energy vibration will raise the frequency of everyone and everything around you.

Learning to raise your vibrational frequency takes practice. To get to the level of doing this with ease is likely to take at least three weeks of repeatedly practising it for most people.

HOW DO I BECOME AN ATTRACTOR?

The second component of the Law of Attraction is aligning ourselves with what we want to create. The Reticular Activating System (RAS) is at the top of the spinal column, the base of your brain, and then extends upwards. All of your senses are linked to this bundle of neurons. The RAS is a filter that makes sure the brain doesn't have to deal with more sensory information than it can handle. It selects the information that is allowed into the conscious mind based on what we focus on and what we identify with. This is a clever system, because we would be overwhelmed if all of the information that is available to us was allowed in. When you imagine what you want and put your brain's RAS to work, it can be the difference between achieving your dreams or living a life of quiet desperation. This is because what we focus on is what the RAS uses to filter awareness into our conscious mind. If you focus on the colour red and glance around to see if there's any red, you will notice it. Try it.

We also need to align our focus and attention with what we want to create, as when we engage with something our energy flows there, we experience it and bring it into reality. We call this accessing quantum intelligence. We create our own reality. By co-creating with the energy around us, we bring the potential of something into reality.

One way of focusing on what we want is to visualize it, imagine that it is already happening and tap into how that feels. Using our creative powers in this way, we have the choice to rewrite our story and manifest the life of our dreams. Sometimes when you think about what you want, you can still have negative feelings and negative emotions around it that you haven't let go of yet and that's why you're not yet attracting what you want into your life.

Can we really believe in a future that we can't see or experience with our senses? YES – we can teach our body emotionally what that future would feel like now. When we are able to elicit the emotional state ahead of the actual experience, we create the emotion of our desire. Our body as the unconscious mind doesn't know the difference between an actual experience in life that creates an emotion and an emotion that we can create by thought alone. To the body, it's exactly the same. Your body will then emotionally live the energetic expression of the quality that the experience will give you in the future, instead of living in our experience from past thoughts. This then creates the vibrational frequency of that emotion and puts the Law of Vibration into motion.

"When you focus on something – the vacation you are going to take, the meeting you are about to go into, the project you want to launch – that focus instantly creates ideas and thought patterns you wouldn't have had otherwise. Even your physiology will respond to an image in your head as if it were reality."

David Allen

But our brain doesn't like the unknown, it likes certainty. So how do we overcome this? Our brain has two operating modes: toward and away. In the toward operating state, when we feel relaxed and open, the brain can see the bigger picture and is open to new and experiencing new things. The Connection Practice is an easy way to access this state.

By using the Connection Practice to access an expanded state first, we are connected not only to our head's logical brain, but also to all of our intelligence, so that we can tune in with our knowing, wisdom and creativity to experience the unknown and what we desire. This helps stop our resistance and it becomes more familiar, training the brain to access future possibility rather than wanting to stay comfortable in the past.

If you can think and envision it, vividly, enough times for your body to experience the feelings, your brain will have already changed to look like the experience has already occurred. As we've discussed earlier, we know that where we focus our attention is what we create. Also, you can rewire your brain just by thinking differently. By adapting and aligning with our desired future, we have used neuroplasticity to create new neural pathways. This new reality becomes hardwired, and that influences future choices, bringing it into reality now. In this way, we get our old self out of the way to allow the new to come in.

What this leads to is the final way of aligning with what we want to create, which is to embody it. The Connection Practice enables us to access a state where we not only align our brain to what we want to create, but also our body. Once we have expanded into a more conscious state of being and set the intention to connect with what we want to create, we can then start to embody it. As our brain changes to believe that we are in that future reality, we begin to emotionally embrace it to such an extent that our body, as the unconscious mind, begins to believe that is it living in that future reality in the present moment. This signals new genes and new pathways so that our body begins to change to look like the experience has already occurred.

As you tune into the unknown with your knowing, your mind and body adapt and align with the future reality, and you become a magnet to the new possibilities. When your body and brain are physically changed to look like the experience has already occurred – this is the moment to relax because the experience is going to find you. It's going to come in a way that you least expect, that surprises you, and leaves no doubt that what you did inside produced the effect outside of you. When you can correlate the changes you've made inside you with the effect produced outside of you, you pay attention to what you did and you'll do it again.

IS YOUR VISION BIG ENOUGH?

We all have our own unique set of gifts and talents and expressing our full potential is using those to the full, which is both pleasurable and rewarding. This is about accessing our own unique genius. How comfortable are you with accepting that you have genius potential?

In order to connect with and be able to sense your own full potential, you need to be in an expanded state and in touch with the energy of your true self. Otherwise your head brain will be in charge and limit your vision, and therefore limit the potential and future possibilities you see for yourself. To create a vision that includes this potential, your thinking has to go beyond your current situation and environment; otherwise, you keep creating the same reality over and over again.

Everything in this world that has been created by humankind started with an idea or vision for it. This vision ignited somebody's passion for creating something new and, when connected and aligned with their potential, was brought into reality.

Every great person in history defined a vision bigger than himself or herself.

The things that have limited what we created in our lives in the past keep us small. We didn't understand how to access the energy of potential. We know that potential is unlimited and that it is only our thoughts that limit it. Actually, potential, like everything else, is energy. It is therefore always available to us in the form of energy and it is up to us to connect to it, engage with it, passionately commit to it and make it real. If you are willing to believe in your unlimited potential, you will start to attract opportunities to manifest it and your life will become rich, magical and full of purpose.

We now set out the key steps to 'Creating an abundant life'. They build on what you have done so far, and then explore the ultimate steps and key secrets to accessing your creative powers so you have the choice to manifest the life of your dreams and unleash this power – not letting life just happen to you, but being the master of your life and a proactive influence.

The steps we have practised so far:

1. Setting intentions – this is the start to creating new pathways and connecting to our vision

2. How to be present and in the moment without the constant chatter in our heads, as we can only create the future from how we are in this moment of now

3. Expanding into a more connected state of being and starting to use that in our relationships with others and ourselves. We can't change anything if we are looking at it from the same state that we created it in – our new state is the secret to manifesting our vision

4. Accessing the state of full connection, where we expand into a more conscious and aware state using all of our true self. It's only from here, we can start to use this awareness to create the life that we desire

The next steps to manifesting:

1. Be in an expanded state of being, where your mind is quiet and you are connected to all of yourself with the Connection Practice, which takes you into the ZOC

2. Set a clear, strong intention to connect with your potential and your vision of what you want to create

3. From here you can easily access your knowing and use this to see and create what your vision and potential is

4. Connect with what you would like to manifest in its final form and embody it; feel what it will be like and live it in your mind's eye. Raise your frequency accordingly – like attracts like

5. Stay focused on the final outcome and trust that what you put out there will become reality. Stay open, not fixed, on how it will come about. Keep your frequency up to the level that you have envisioned

6. Hold your vision and follow any hunches, instincts, intuition and feelings that take you toward what you desire. The clues may be subtle: a word, images, an ah-ha moment. Keep looking for them

7. Celebrate each step as you see it materializing! We're not joking – it's an important step to acknowledge and enjoy your success. This reinforces and imprints on your subconscious that it is happening and helps bring it through into reality. As we embody this new way of being, we attract more of that into our life

Experience the exercise to
manifest an abundant life

The exercises in this chapter are to support you in putting what you learn into practice. The best way to experience them is by being guided by us using the audio versions which you can download using the link or QR code shared. Alternatively, you can do them by recording them on your phone and playing them back or by using the explanation in the text.

Exercise 14
Manifesting an abundant life

First, we'll be using your creativity to connect to and access a greater level of your potential and a vision that inspires you in an exercise starting with the first three steps to manifesting, so that you can create abundance in your life.

Find a quiet place to try this out, somewhere you feel that you can relax and not be disturbed.

Step 1

- Set a clear, strong intention to connect with your potential and to manifest a future vision of abundance that is aligned with your purpose and the authentic true you
- First, expand to a state of full connection
- Feel your feet on the ground and your spine aligned
- Close your eyes
- Notice any sensations in your body and take a moment to allow it to relax
- Bring your attention to the energy surrounding your body and feel for balance in it
- Take a big breath in and as you sigh your breath out, let go of anything that gets in the way of you being in touch with your potential and vision. Repeat this letting go a few times
- Now take a deep breath down into your belly connecting your head, heart and gut brains as you connect yourself up and slow down and become calmer
- From the centre point in your chest, start to imagine a line going up through your body and all the way to the centre of the radiant sun
- Now come back down the line into your body and down all the way to the centre of the earth
- Feel aligned between the sun and the earth
- Sense the energy in your heart centre starting to open and expand into your body

○ Allow this energy to expand beyond your body, merging with the energy around you, getting bigger and bigger

○ Expand that vibrant energy way out to encompass the whole earth, out past the planets and connecting to the infinite universe

○ Expand out as far as you can possibly imagine, to where you have no edges and are fully connected to everything and observe how it feels to be in your expanded energy field. From this expanded place, you can tune into everything and sense the energy within and around you

○ Expand right to the outer edges of the universe, allowing yourself to expand into a really infinite place of possibilities, a miraculous place where you are connected to the knowing and intelligence that is inside you and all around you

○ From here, set a strong intention and call upon your awareness to tune into, connect with and bring into reality the greatest potential for yourself

○ Now start to feel your passion for this and allow it to flow and fuel you as you go through this visualization and connect with your desire, potential and vision for an abundant life

○ Expand and open yourself to your highest purpose. Allow the energy of what wants to happen through you to come to you

Step 2

○ From here, you can easily access your knowing and use this to see and create what your vision and potential is. Imagine what your future will be like when you have what you want. Remember that you have no limitations on time, money, energy, skills, etc.

○ Tune into your imagination. It's like a computer connected up to the internet or like a radio that you can tune into. Imagine tuning into the energy of your abundant future and have a conversation with that energy to find out what is there. Assume it will talk to you and let you know what it is and what your potential is, because after all it's really you talking to yourself here. As you tune into that abundant future, use all of your senses to experience it; you may have images, textures, or smells come to you to take you there

○ Let all of this come into your knowing and give you a sense of that future. Trust whatever comes. Breathe it through, partner with it. Let it come from the expanded space and stream through you

○ Think about times when you have felt this energy before; maybe there is a special place where you feel this energy

○ It may be that today you won't get anything. Give this connection time to develop

Step 3

○ Connect with what you would like to manifest in its final form and embody it; feel what it will be like and live it in your mind's eye

○ Imagine yourself in that future and make all your senses come alive. You want to feel this with all your senses

○ See what it's like to have what you want. Smell the aromas around you. Feel it with your hands and your body. Make it as real as you possibly can. See this as real, no limitations — where are you, what are you doing or saying, how are you being?

○ Now tune into your body and notice how you feel in your body. If there are any sensations of fear, raise your energy to replace it with feelings of exuberance, confidence, joy and certainty

○ Feel as though your cup is overflowing, unquestioning, and with an expectation that you have everything you need right here and now. A deep sense of knowing that everything you need will flow into your life

○ Embody this energy; feel it spreading, infusing throughout your body from your heart; allow this vibe to fill your body, allow every one of the 70 trillion cells in your body to be bathed with this energy and say YES to it

○ Be it — become the high energy of abundance

○ Say it out loud: "My life is abundant"

○ Take a moment to imagine all the wonderful experiences that you will have when you have what you want. What is it you are going to do with this? What kind of people will you share this with? And what physical sensations and emotions are you feeling, what emotions are coming up for you? Pay attention

○ Notice what that feels like emotionally. Maybe you are buzzing with happiness, joy and exhilaration. Your whole body is vibrating with that and that is an energy you can create any time. Let your energy field start to light up with this vibe. Imagine stepping into that energy and let it infuse all the cells of your body. Allow yourself to walk around as that, feeling it as you walk vibrantly in the world

○ Now pulsate this energy out into the universe, see it flowing out and expanding into the field of energy around you and farther out into the universe, sending a very clear message to the universe that says: "Yes, I want more of this." See it making its imprint and then imagine it rebounding back to you multiplied and showering you

○ Say to the universe: "Thank you for bringing this about"

○ Gently open your eyes and make a note in your journal

"Be the change you wish to see in the world."
Gandhi

It's our responsibility to start creating and manifesting now! We are far more influential than we realize. All energy is inter-connected, so a butterfly flapping its wings on one side of the world may set off a chain reaction or ripple effect that results in a tornado on the other side of the world. This means we can make conscious choices about how we live our lives and the sort of impact we want to have in the world.

In Chapter 6 we discussed the degree to which each one of us can live from our highest self and see the highest potential in all of our relationships. This affects not only our own experience of life, but also that of our loved ones, our friends, our work associates, the strangers we interact with, and in many ways the extended network of people we're all connected with. It doesn't take much to see we are all influencing each other in some way directly or indirectly by the way we choose to be in the world.

Expressing our unique talents creates abundance. Through our energy, we have an unlimited capacity to send out ripples that will help the planet and its inhabitants move away from fear, hostility and unrest to love compassion, peace and joy. This is what it means to have a vision that makes a difference to future generations and the planet.

Now we will do steps 4 and 5 of the manifesting process, which are about keeping your vision alive in your life, celebrating it and letting it make a difference to the world.

Step 4

- Trust, surrender and allow what you put out there to become reality. Stay open, not fixed, on how it will come about — let go of the detail. Keep the intention alive in your daily life by feeling the energy of it already being present in your life and by energizing this intention every day. Stay focused on the final outcome and keep it alive in your daily life

- Hold your vision and physically follow any instincts, intuition and feelings that take you toward what you desire. The clues may be subtle words, images or ah-ha moments

- In your morning Connection Practice, bring this image in and let yourself feel the energy of what you are creating, seeing and feeling the vision of abundance — embody it. Trusting that it will come to you, be excited and watch out for each big or little step as it starts to manifest in your life and remember it won't come in the form that you expect, but in a much better way for you and everyone

- Throughout the day, pay attention to your thoughts and your feelings. Notice any time that you feel something that is not aligned with your vision and change your thoughts immediately until you feel your desired energy, so that becomes your dominant energy and therefore becomes your reality

○ Practise tuning into your body and what you are feeling throughout the day. Notice what you are thinking when you are feeling certain things, because you want to consciously create more positive feelings and associated energy and its vibration throughout your body. The more positive you feel, the more you will attract your vision and the circumstances that bring it about

○ For instance, let's say you want more money because you want more freedom. You can choose to create more activities in your life that give you more freedom. You can choose to have feelings of freedom, even right now, so that becomes your dominant energy. So you may choose to carve out an hour a day that is unrestricted and unstructured and you have the freedom to do whatever you want. You may choose to take up running so you have the feeling of freedom. Anything that is going to generate those feelings for you right now, before your circumstances change, will actually help you to change your circumstances

○ Remember every day to watch your thoughts, watch your feelings and choose to create positive experiences for yourself

Step 5

○ Celebrate and raise your energy to gratitude. Doing this as you see each step materializing ensures that you attract more to be grateful for! It's an important step to acknowledge and enjoy your success. This reinforces and imprints on your subconscious that it is happening and helps bring it through into reality. As we embody this new way of being and put the energy vibe of it out there, we attract more of that into our life

○ Find different ways to do this using your creativity and focus You may enjoy feeling this energy by dancing it!

Our willingness to give what we seek keeps the abundance of the universe circulating. Creating a better world starts with each of us as individuals wanting to live a life that matters, connecting to a bigger purpose than ourselves and using our whole being to bring it into reality. Many of us are already on this path. The good news is there is a massive movement of people who are making this choice. This is one of the aspects of our work that we most love!

"Our presence is enough to light the way for others; it can uplift them and guide them on their path. We can become the spark that lights the fire and contribute to collective change by making conscious choices about how we behave and act in the world, benefiting everyone and everything."

Deepak Chopra

In short
KEY CONCEPTS FOR CREATING ABUNDANCE IN YOUR LIFE

- The Law of Vibration states that everything that exists has an energetic frequency; we have our own unique vibration, which is created from our thoughts and intentions, feelings and emotions
- The Law of Attraction states that 'like attracts like'; become an attractor – whatever frequency you are vibrating, you will attract into your life
- You are far more influential than you realize; don't let life just happen to you, be the master of your life and a proactive influence, expressing your unique talents creates abundance

HOW TO CREATE ABUNDANCE DAY TO DAY

- Complete steps 1 to 3 of the manifesting abundance Exercise 14 (page 189)
- In your morning Connection Practice, repeat steps 4 and 5 of the manifesting abundance Exercise 14
- Here they are again to remind you:
  - Let yourself feel the energy of what you are creating, seeing and feeling the vision of what you desire – embody it. Trusting that it will come to you, be excited and watch out for each big or little step as it starts to manifest in your life and remember it won't come in the form that you expect but in a much better way for you and everyone
  - Throughout the day, pay attention to your thoughts and your feelings, notice any time you are feeling something that is not aligned with your vision and change your thoughts until you feel your desired energy so that it becomes your dominant vibration and therefore becomes your reality

- As you tune into what you are feeling throughout the day, notice what you are thinking when you are feeling certain things, because you want to consciously create more positive feelings and associated energy vibe throughout your body. Because the more positive you feel, the more you will attract your vision and the circumstances that bring it about
- Stay focused on the final outcome and keep it alive in your daily life. Trust that what you put out there will become reality. Stay open and not fixed on how it will come about
- Hold your vision and physically follow any instincts, intuitions, feelings that take you toward what you desire. The clues may be subtle: a word, an image, an ah-ha moment

- Celebrate each step as you see it materializing! We're not joking – it's an important step to acknowledge and enjoy your success; this reinforces and imprints on your subconscious that it is happening and helps bring it through into reality. As we embody this new way of being, we attract more of that into our life. Find different ways to do this using your creativity and focus

Try it out for yourself! What are the first steps you intend to take to integrate this into your daily life? Write them down.

Your Reflections

CHAPTER 9

Transforming
your life

"If you want to awaken all of humanity, then awaken all of yourself.
If you want to eliminate the suffering in the world, then eliminate all
that is dark and negative about yourself. Truly the greatest gift you
have to give is that of your own self-transformation."
Wang Fou

HOW TO CONNECT WITH ENERGY AND ALLOW IT TO FLOW TO TRANSFORM YOUR LIFE

Can you see yourself sitting on top of a mountain with crossed legs, meditating for days in order to find enlightenment? Is that even something that you believe is available to you? Even if it were, would you want to put the effort in to get it?

If you were with us during a week in spring 2006, you would have seen us at a silent retreat in the UK countryside, sitting facing each other for hours repeating the question "Who am I?" and waiting for an answer! Eventually Penny was heard to exclaim, "I am love!" Shortly after, Sue followed with a more incredulous statement of "I am light!" Apparently, we had blasted through our ego shield and had a glimpse of our true essence, which was not the outcome for many of the other people attending.

Penny was ecstatically happy by her revelation, but getting the "I am light" realization freaked Sue out. She resisted it, saying that it can't be true, as only higher beings like God and Buddha are light. After some additional support, she gradually came to accept this. Once we had connected with this deepest part of who we are – our true self – our identity and experience of ourselves were forever transformed.

We now know that this possibility is available to all of us and we certainly don't have to sit on top of a mountain meditating for days to get there! The first step, though, is to believe it.

*"The essential lesson I have learned in life is to just be yourself.
Treasure the magnificent being that you are and recognize first
and foremost that you're not here as a human being only.
You're a spiritual being having a human experience."*
Wayne Dyer

Core Beliefs: I am light and love and I radiate happiness and joy.

WHAT IS TRANSFORMATION?

Transformation can be defined as a change or alteration, especially a radical one (*Collins Dictionary*). It implies that you are making a fundamental change or changing something or someone at the core. Transformation involves shifting from one state of being to another (like the caterpillar to the butterfly). It's about how we are being, not what we are doing.

Our mindset is multilayered and the deepest, most unconscious layers are:

- Identity
- Purpose
- Values
- Attitudes and beliefs
- Talent/gifts

Much of these unconscious aspects of our mindset are hardwired during the first seven years of life, when our brains are like a sponge and take on the beliefs and attitudes of the adults and environment around us. This is what we have referred to as our default mindset. As we journey through life, we may start to address some of the limitations of our default mindset and rewire them using neuroplasticity so that our values, beliefs and behaviours are more aligned with what we want for ourselves, as adults.

Eventually some of you will take this right to the core, to your identity and purpose – this is called a transformation.

Having spent five years in Singapore in her dream job, travelling the world, with many friends, Penny had her first baby and was looking forward to going home to her family in the UK when her husband was offered his dream job in Australia! Penny then found herself on the other side of the world with her new baby, feeling very much alone, with no friends or family and unable to work.

For a period of six months, she struggled and felt the lowest she had ever felt, as the things that had given her purpose, been important to her and supported her, were no longer there. She cried herself to sleep many nights, desperate and low, not managing to express what she was going through and feeling powerless. This was probably the root cause of her Hashimoto's disease.

However difficult this was, it turned out to be her opportunity to transform and recreate her life. The unconditional love that she had found for her baby had blown her heart wide open. She started the journey of recreating her life by finding the things that made her heart sing: relationships (another baby!), adventures, studying, learning to fly. By finding her passions and creating from the inside out, she reinvented herself. She found new meaning and started the journey back to her true self.

Three years later she moved back to the UK when a best friend committed suicide. She was in disbelief, as he was one of the most loved and successful people she knew. This devastating event kick-started her quest to understand how human beings work. Many other synchronicities followed. She was trying to decide what work she wanted to do back in the UK when she met a homeless grandmother in a train station – she couldn't imagine how terrifying it would be to be homeless and this started the next phase in her career, working for a housing trust. She had found a new purpose for her life.

HOW DOES TRANSFORMATION HAPPEN?

As human beings, we are living systems. If we look at nature, we can see that change happens naturally – it just emerges in response to the environment. The same would be true of human beings if we allowed it to happen. Nobody teaches us that life is meant to be a series of transformations. These transformations can't be planned; our bodies and the universe give us signals (often in the form of wake-up calls) when the time is right. Very often, though, we are so busy that we miss these signals.

If we don't embrace our ongoing transformation, we get stuck and fight life instead of embracing and flowing with it. As a result, we stay small and are unable to realize our potential. Going through transformation is a journey, as shown in the diagram.

The transformation journey

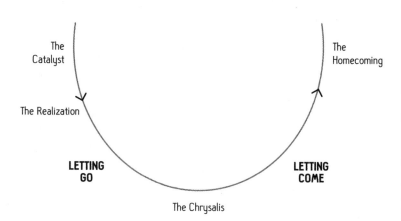

The Chrysalis

THE STAGES IN THE
TRANSFORMATION JOURNEY

There are seven stages in the transformation journey – the six depicted in the diagram and a seventh, overarching stage.

The catalyst

Something happens to trigger the transformation. The catalyst for transformation can be a wake-up call such as a serious illness (often related to unfinished business from the past or blocked energy in the body), divorce, bereavement, burn-out, breakdown, etc. It can also be that several areas of your life crash at the same time, and you realize that a radical shift needs to happen.

"My father passed away last year and I was much sadder than I thought I would be, as we had a difficult relationship. My father wasn't able to fulfil his dream and so he was living it through me. Now he has gone it feels as if I have the space to live my own life and to find out what I want to give my heart and soul to." Male former advertising executive, early 50s.

This often happens during the self-actualizing stage of development, where there is a search for meaning and purpose. This stage for many people occurs around the age of 40 and creates a mid-life crisis as the catalyst for transformation. Transformation, though, can occur at any age and any time and certainly each time we transition from one stage of development to the next (Chapter 2), there is the likelihood of transformation happening. Transformation provides an opportunity to grow beyond whatever is the catalyst.

Since 2003, when she got divorced, Sue dedicated herself to bringing up her two children. Having previously been very strongly identified with her work, even though she was still working, being a mother was a key aspect of her identity. When the children grew up and left home in their early 20s, Sue felt bereft and abandoned.

She worked with healing practitioners to liberate those emotions and see the potential opening up for her as she entered the empty-nest stage of her life. The vision for this next stage of her life is to make it the best decade yet. Her vision includes travelling, relationships and fulfilling her purpose through her work. Each threshold that we cross into a new life phase brings with it grief for what we are letting go of from the past and the possibility of joy from what is emerging.

The realization

Often it takes a while for us to develop a conscious awareness that things need to change radically. Even when we have a wake-up call, it may take us a while to realize its implications. Some people never do. They deny themselves the opportunity to transform and grow by allowing their own or other people's fears to hold them back.

Many of Sue's coaching clients come for coaching to address a particular issue and during the course of the coaching the deeper, more transformational reason that they need coaching emerges.

Letting go

This phase of the journey involves overcoming our limiting beliefs from childhood and clearing blocked emotions that get in the way of transformation. This is a process of becoming aware of your current beliefs, values and identity, and letting go of aspects that no longer serve you. It is about clearing out the old and creating space for the new.

During this stage of the transformation journey, there can be a range of emotions such as shock, denial, anger and sadness. Only when you get to a feeling of acceptance can you start to let go of the past and open to the possibilities of the future.

"There is a lot of grief I need to get rid of. I need to cry, but I am trying to be strong for my daughter." Female senior manager, public sector, early 40s.

The chrysalis

For a period, you are in limbo land. A place of not knowing. This is where you are no longer who you were because you have let go of that identity and neither are you who you are becoming. People often talk about feeling lost during this phase, which can last for weeks, months or even years. It is like the caterpillar going into the chrysalis.

"Work was my whole identity. I came to judgments too quickly and didn't listen. I made people feel distressed. Once I stopped and reflected, I realized I didn't like who I had become. I had become selfish. There was a lot of hurt and pain in that realization. I realize now that I had lost myself. Since I have been off work, I have just slept for nine months. During this time, old anxieties have surfaced; my head has felt heavy and cluttered and I have not been able to absorb anything. I think the sleep has been helping me to heal. Meditation has helped me to start to get back in touch with the real me." Female senior manager, public sector, early 40s.

During this period, you need to get the insights and learning to help you grow into who you are becoming. It is a stage during which you might need outside support to help you to break through into the new version of yourself that is emerging. You will come across people and information that will guide you as to what the next step is that you need to take. No one can tell you how to navigate this period, but if you notice the signs you will be guided one step at a time. Everyone has their own journey and it is about finding your own way. People often say that you have to break down to break through and if you hold onto that thought the difficulties you may encounter during this stage can be seen from a different perspective.

> *"As you start to walk out on the way,*
> *the way appears."*
> **Rumi**

Letting come

Eventually you get to a point where you are ready to emerge as the new version of yourself. You start to see a vision for the future and get clear on who you are and what you stand for. You then go out and try out this new you in day-to-day life.

"It feels as if the stars are all aligned now for me to step into the new me. I want to take advantage of this alignment to jump forward." Male, former advertising executive, early 50s.

The homecoming

Eventually you feel comfortable with the new you and it becomes normal. You have a deep feeling of coming back to who you really are and relish the opportunity to start to live life from that place. You feel as if you have come home.

"I feel surprisingly peaceful; it feels completely normal to be like this. It is as if that is how it should have always been. It is the energy of going where you should have always been. It is like coming back home." Male, former advertising executive, early 50s.

Evolution

As human beings, we continually transform as we go through life. After the first big transformation you experience, you come to realize that transformation is not a one-off experience. You start to understand the signs when another one is starting and you openly embrace it, knowing there is something better on the other side. You know when to ask for support and, to a greater extent than previously, can support yourself through it. In this way, it just becomes a way of evolving and growing on your journey through life.

The ultimate level of transformation could be seen as the shift from our ego state back to an energetic state of oneness with everything.

Where are you on the transformation curve of your life?

USING EMOTIONS TO FUEL TRANSFORMATION

One of the ways of recognizing when transformation is occurring is to be aware of the emotions involved at each stage of the journey, as shown in the diagram.

Transforming emotion

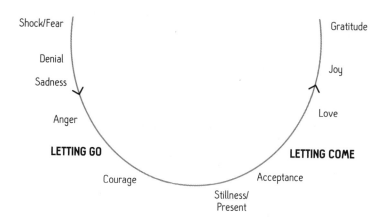

What if those emotions could be used to fuel your journey?

There are five aspects to be aware of:

- Emotions are energy in motion
- Emotions help us realize our potential
- Negative emotions close you down
- Acceptance allows emotions to flow and you to transform
- You can choose to consciously change your emotional vibration

Emotion is energy in motion

We have said that everything is energy, and emotion is no exception. E-motion is energy in motion.

On the transformational journey, the initial emotions are shock, fear, denial, sadness, anger. Eventually courage kicks in to move you through the chrysalis phase. Only when you get to a centred, still place where you are present and can accept your emotions can you use them to move forward through the transformation and experience the joy and gratitude of coming home.

Seeing the potential in emotions

In the Western world, we have been conditioned to believe that emotions have to be either suppressed or resisted, especially negative emotions. They've been seen as unwanted and unhelpful. We tend to focus instead on rational thought using our head brain. This is starting to change with recent teachings around emotional intelligence pointing to being more responsible and open about emotions because they have an important role to play in our success.

As events take place in the outside world, we experience them through our senses. We sense the world, convert the information and transmit the data through electrical nerve impulses. These become impressions that our mind and heart receive and experience, and, as such, they have an impact on our feelings and emotions. What if, instead of resisting and suppressing it, we could use the energy of emotion as the fuel for realizing more of our potential?

Perceiving emotion as the energy of potential allows us to tap into it and use it to help us to grow and transform. Let's explore how seeing emotion in this way changes how we see some of our core emotions:

- Sadness is the opportunity to let go of something
- Fear is the opportunity to transform
- Anger is the opportunity for feeling our passion

STOPPING NEGATIVE EMOTIONS
FROM CLOSING YOU DOWN

If we are not ready to accept negative emotions, then we react by entering a state of survival or we block the emotion. You innately know how to close down to avoid being too receptive and sensitive to the different energies coming in and causing fear. When you close down to protect yourself, you become constricted and contracted rather than expanded, and you block the flow of energy. It can be helpful to imagine that there is a channel that runs up through the centre of your body, connecting your energy centres and allowing energy to flow through you. When you close your energy centres, this channel becomes blocked and energy can't flow through you.

How does this happen?

If you were to observe this process of closing down, you would notice that there is constant inner chatter going on in your mind. It is like a running commentary on what is happening around you. The mind-talk happens because there is a build-up of nervous, fearful or desire-based energy inside that needs to be released, and talking releases energy. What you end up experiencing through the mind-talk is a personal interpretation of the world, which allows you to buffer reality. You recreate the world within your mind because you can control your mind, whereas you can't control the world.

Why does closing down limit our potential?

The universe is energy, and we are a part of this universal energy field. We also have an inner energy that is referred to as chi (or qi), life-force energy or spirit that you may have experienced in Exercise 9 (page 134). This inner energy flows up the channel that goes from the base of your spine up to the crown of your head, connecting all of your energy centres. It can heal and transform you if it is allowed to flow. For this to be possible, you need to keep your inner channel free from blocked energy and emotions.

You have the potential to feel emotions and use them as the energy of transformation, experiencing the high-frequency emotions such as love and joy associated with coming home to who you really are.

You might be thinking that this is easier said than done. When we are not aware of how this happens, we are not able to make conscious choices about opening up and closing down. This happens unconsciously as our unfinished, stored past experiences get stimulated/triggered by different events. If negative impressions from the past are triggered, we close; if positive ones are triggered, we stay open. All kinds of things can cause us to open and close. Since closing down has such a profound effect on your life, is this something that you want to allow to happen to you? The good news is that 'closing' is a habit and as we have already learned, we can rewire our brains and consciously create new habits (Chapter 4).

As you start to recognize the signs of closing down, you can interrupt that pattern and choose to stay open, setting a different context for your emotion, welcoming it as energy passing through and a prompt moving you toward your potential. Each time you do this, you are creating new wiring in your brain, and ultimately staying open becomes the habit instead of closing down, allowing life-force energy to flow. The associated feelings of enthusiasm, joy and love will make you want to experience it more. You realize that you don't have to shut down anymore and that it is better to stay open no matter what happens on the outside, and the Connection Practice enables this.

The more you learn to stay open, the more energy can flow into you and through you.

This affects other people as they pick up on your energy. You become a source of light and energize those around you. The key to this is to keep your inner life-force energy flowing so that you can transform and have a transformational effect on others.

SHIFTING TO AN ACCEPTANCE MINDSET

A key stage on the transformation journey is to reach a state of acceptance. It allows emotions to flow and you to transform.

This means accepting that everyone's journey through life involves going through some challenging times and situations. Constant change is a feature of modern life and for many of us that is seen as a challenge to be avoided and controlled. If we try to avoid these challenges, we diminish our resilience, restrict our life experiences and limit our potential.

It is also about accepting the truth rather than denying it. Denying the truth is like looking out of the window, seeing that it is snowing and telling yourself, "It can't be snowing." It is snowing and denying it won't solve any of the problems it may cause.

We are human beings, and we are going to experience many different emotions. By accepting your emotions, you are accepting what it is to be a human being, that emotions are our friends. When you accept your emotions, you accept the truth of your situation and don't expend energy resisting or pushing the emotion away. Once you have acknowledged the emotion, you can move beyond it and choose the behaviours that are aligned with your goals and values. You also learn about your emotional landscape. You learn to recognize different emotions and allow them to be integrated into your life.

A bonus is that when you accept a negative emotion and see it as energy with a message to convey, it tends to lose its destructive power. Imagine you are swimming in the sea and get caught in a current, and you are being dragged out to sea. There is no point trying to swim against the current. You need to let go, let the current take you and then when it weakens swim back to shore. The same is true of a powerful emotion: accept it and it will run its course.

Accepting and feeling your emotions helps them to pass more quickly.

> *"If you allow yourself to feel something fully,*
> *it will only last 7–12 seconds."*
> **Josh Pais, actor**

Also, allowing yourself to experience negative emotions allows you to fully experience positive emotions. People who suppress emotions such as fear and anger are unable to feel other more positive emotions fully, as they are afraid that in so doing the fear or anger will burst out in an uncontrollable way. Accepting emotions is a skill that can be learned. A good way is to think of your emotions as passing clouds, visible but not a part of you. The Connection Practice helps you to always see the blue sky and the sun behind the clouds.

Use the Connection Practice
to accept your emotions and
transform them into potential

The best way to experience this and the following exercise is by being guided by us using the audio versions, which you can download using the link or QR code shared. Alternatively, you can do them by recording them on your phone and playing them back or by using the explanation in the text.

Acceptance is a transitional emotion between the negative low-vibe emotions and the positive high-vibe emotions (see the 'Range of emotional frequencies' table on page 43). Acceptance means allowing unwanted thoughts, feelings and urges to come and go without struggling with them. It is the willingness and ability to acknowledge, accept and experience a negative emotion rather than suppress it. It requires letting go of control and maintaining a nonjudgmental mindset. It's about surrendering, trusting in life and allowing it to flow.

There is a lot of evidence to show that accepting your negative emotions leads to better emotional resilience, fewer symptoms of depression and anxiety and also helps stop you projecting them onto others, so it is well worth practising Exercise 15.

Exercise 15
Accepting emotions and transforming them into potential

In this exercise, you will build on the exercise in Chapter 4 on letting go of blocked emotions. Really going for this will help you to get the most out of it. Do it in a way that works for you, so if you are asked to stand up and you are uncomfortable, please feel free to do it sitting down.

There may be some language you haven't heard or seen before – just trust the process, trust yourself and trust us!

Go for it! It will have a transformational effect on your life and others too.

Step 1: Setting intentions
○ First, find a place where you will not be disturbed
○ Create a safe space where you can just be yourself; there is no right or wrong, whatever you feel is just right for you
○ Close your eyes now and tune into any area of your life where you experience negative emotions and a low energy. It might be an area where you feel blocked and where you don't feel good, maybe stressed or fearful. Take a moment to bring to mind a time when you have felt like that
○ Set an intention to let go of any negative emotions and shift to acceptance. Imagine that amazing possibility for yourself right there in front of you and say YES to it

Step 2: Use the Connection Practice to let go of blocked emotions
Posture and balance are important for our body, as it functions better when it is in alignment. Whether we are standing, sitting or lying down, posture and balance enable the body to function at its best. To encourage this:
○ Lengthen your spine and open your chest, feel a posture of upright-ness and openness, feeling supported with a sense of integrity and alignment

- Relax your jaw and shoulders – let gravity have them
- Soften your heart and relax your pelvic floor
- Start to allow yourself to become aware of what's going on for you right now in this moment
- Take a moment to observe what is going on in your thoughts, your feelings and your body; notice any sensations with a sense of acceptance

Extending beyond your physical body is your energy body, which is a sphere that surrounds you. You are now going to feel for balance within your energy body.

- Repeat: "I allow myself to wonder, what it would be like if my energy was equal and even at the back and front of my body?"
- It may help to imagine your energy field as a colour or texture
- "If it was equal and even to the right and left sides? And if it was equal and even above my head and below me?"
- Take a moment to feel for that balance. Allow yourself to rest in the safety of your field and trust it to support you
- Call upon your awareness to notice your breath. Take a moment to notice where it is in your body
- Now bring to mind the negative energy that has felt blocked, tune back into it, remember when you last felt it
- Feel where it is in your body, what does it feel like – colour, texture, image – then acknowledge it and give yourself permission to let it go
- Start by taking some big breaths in through your nose then sighing it out through your mouth, bringing this energy up and out
- Really let yourself feel it, breathe into it and then breathe it out; if sounds need to come as you do this, just let them come
- Let go of anything that is blocking you: breathe it out, keep letting go, coming back to who you really are. Do this cleansing breath a few times. Really let all that blocked emotion go
- Now use your breath to become really present; inhale for a count of six, pause until your body naturally wants to breathe out and exhale for a count of six. As you breathe in slowly and fully through your nose,

allow your belly to swell and expand. The belly is the seat of your sense of presence, knowing and deep confidence. Breathe your energy down from your head into your heart and gut brain to connect all of yourself up

○ Repeat this breath two more times

○ Feel yourself calming down and a sense of stillness, allowing everything to be as it is, accepting what is

Step 3: Getting to acceptance

○ Now start to breathe in the energy of acceptance — allow your awareness to feel and tune into the energy of acceptance

○ As you do so, say: "I feel acceptance, I experience a sense of trust and surrender to what is, allowing life to flow. I feel a sense of calm and that things will work out for the best. I love and accept myself exactly as I am. I am accepted by others and I accept them"

○ Let this feeling of acceptance spread throughout your body, bathing each and every one of the 70 trillion cells in your body in its soothing energy

Step 4: Seeing the potential for transformation

○ Now tune back into the area of your life that came to mind at the start of this exercise and see it from this place of acceptance. Notice how this transforms your experience of this situation. Keep tuning into the situation and ask yourself what potential the situation offers you. Trust your knowing and whatever comes to you. You may get images, words, sensations — just trust whatever comes. Really get in touch with what the potential is for you on your transformational journey

○ Once you consciously understand what that potential is, ask yourself are you ready to choose it, then own it and say YES to it

○ Imagine what it would be like to have realized that potential and embody how it feels. Step into it as if it is happening now. What do you see, hear, feel?

- Open your eyes and write down or speak into your phone's recorder what came to you about this potential and what wants to happen now on your transformational journey
- Using acceptance in this way will help you to acknowledge and accept negative situations and emotions as they occur, see the potential in them and transform how you see them so that you can realize that potential

CONSCIOUSLY CHANGING YOUR EMOTIONAL VIBRATION

Once we accept that emotions are energy in motion and it is human to experience them, we are ready to consciously choose them.

How do we do that?

David R. Hawkins, MD, an internationally renowned psychiatrist and consciousness researcher, developed a scale of consciousness (more details in his book, *Power vs Force*) showing the full range of emotions, from the most negative to the most positive, along with their vibrational frequency (see Chapter 2). Negative emotions have a low vibrational frequency and are experienced as heavy energy. Positive emotions vibrate at a higher frequency and are lighter. As human beings, we are constantly vibrating, and our frequency is determined by our emotions.

We can choose to shed the weight of our heavy emotions and stop carrying that baggage and heavy load around by moving toward positive emotions.

Our natural state is to be happy and in a space of love. It requires more energy and effort to feel bad than it does to feel good. So by changing your vibrational frequency and moving toward more positive emotions, you are simply *undoing* stuff that keeps you from naturally feeling good.

Let's apply the emotional frequency information to the transformation curve.

Transforming emotion

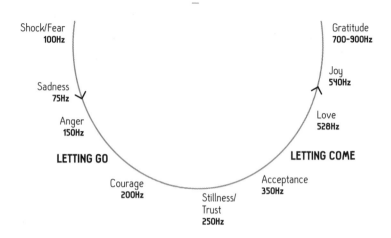

As discussed earlier, our emotions operate at different frequencies:

- Fear at the thought of the transformational journey ahead of us vibrates as 100 Hz, and it is usually experienced as worry, anxiety or panic
- As we start to let go of our old identity, we may feel a sense of loss and dip to an even lower frequency to experience grief and sadness (75 Hz)
- Anger comes next (150 Hz). This is a high-energy emotion and if used constructively can fuel resolve and determination
- As we move on in our journey, we move up the scale of emotions
- We tap into our true power and begin to find the courage (200 Hz) to move through the transformation. Courage brings empowerment
- We then start to experience trust (250 Hz) This is mainly about self-trust, being neutral, letting go of either resistance or attachment and not being judgmental. It also involves trusting that even though the journey feels challenging, it is worth it, as there is something better on the other side

- Eventually we reach acceptance (350 Hz). Transformation starts to happen here, as we realize that we are the source of our own happiness and that we have the power within us to bring about our transformation. It is about reclaiming your own power. This is the frequency we accessed in Exercise 15 earlier in this chapter
- As we allow our new identity to emerge, we move up to the healing frequency of unconditional love (540 Hz). We feel inner serenity and compassion and at the same time feel more alive and full of joy
- Finally, we feel gratitude (700–900 Hz) for the learning, growth and potential realized through the transformational journey. Having gratitude raises your vibrational frequency because it makes you aware of all the things you love and how abundant your life is

Even when experiencing the negative emotions associated with the early stages of transformation, you can choose at any time to raise your emotional frequency and attract more of that energy into your life.

Use the Connection Practice to raise your vibration and bring the new you into reality.

As you move around the transformation curve, letting go of blocked emotions, you eventually get to a state of acceptance of the transformation that is happening in you. The next stage is to bring that transformation through into reality by moving into a higher vibration. The high-vibe zone goes from happiness, through love and peace, to gratitude and oneness. Exercise 16 supports you in getting into full connection, accessing the high-vibe zone and allowing the new you to become reality.

Exercise 16
Raising your vibe to bring the new you into reality

As we said in Chapter 8, raising your vibrational frequency takes practice, but it is well worth persevering until you master this ability, as it is key to embracing transformation in your life and bringing through more of your potential into reality.

1. Set intentions

○ Close your eyes now and set your intention to experience a state of full connection, access the high-vibe zone and bring the new you into reality. Imagine that possibility for yourself and say YES to it

2. Balance and posture

Posture and balance is important, as our bodies function best when they are in alignment whether we are standing, sitting or lying down.

○ Lengthen your spine and open your chest, feel a posture of uprightness and openness, feeling supported with a sense of integrity and alignment

○ Relax your jaw and shoulders – let gravity have them

○ Soften your heart and relax your pelvic floor

○ Start to allow yourself to become aware of what's going on for you right now in this moment

○ Take a moment to observe what is going on in your thoughts, your feelings and your body; notice any sensations with a sense of acceptance

○ Extending beyond your physical body is your energy body. You are now going to feel for balance within your energy body

○ Repeat: "I allow myself to wonder what it would be like if my energy was equal and even at the back and front of my body?"

○ If it helps you can imagine your energy field as a colour or texture

○ "If it was equal and even to the right and left sides? And if it was equal and even above my head and below me?"

○ Take a moment to feel for that balance. Allow yourself to rest in the safety of your field and trust it to support you

3. Conscious breathing – accessing mindful connection

○ Call upon your awareness to notice your breath. Take a moment to notice where it is in your body
○ Start by taking some big breaths in through your nose, then sighing it out through your mouth, letting go of anything that you don't need that is stopping you being present right here and now; keep letting go, coming back to who you really are. Do this cleansing breath a few times
○ Inhale for a count of six, pause until your body naturally wants to breathe out and exhale for a count of six. As you breathe in slowly and fully through your nose, allow your belly to swell and expand. The belly is the seat of your sense of presence, knowing and deep confidence
○ Breathe your energy down from your head into your heart and gut brain to connect all of yourself up
○ Repeat this two more times
○ Feel a stillness emerging in you, with a sense of acceptance of who you are becoming and how your life is flowing

4. Deepening through centring, alignment and grounding

○ Bring your attention to the centre point of your chest and imagine a line going up through your throat, behind your eyes and out through the crown of your head
○ Then imagine this line extending up through the building that you are in, up through the sky, through the atmosphere of the earth and all the way to the centre of the sun
○ Feel yourself open up and enjoy the beautiful golden light energy and the generous warmth of the sun for a moment or two
○ Then start to move your attention back down this line, back into your body through the crown of your head. Slowly move down behind your eyes, through your throat, through your heart, solar plexus and belly, down into your pelvis and out through your tailbone

○ Keep following the line down your legs and through your feet into mother earth and get in touch with her deep red-hot molten core swirling with life-force energy. Feel grounded with your feet firmly rooted

○ Bringing some of that life-force energy with you, move your attention slowly back up the line, back into your body and connect with your life-force energy at the base of your spine

○ Move this energy up through your inner channel that runs through the core of your body through your energy centres until you reach the crown of your head, awakening your life-force energy and letting it flow freely

5. Expansion – accessing full connection

○ Now move that energy down into the heart centre in your chest and see it as a vibrating ball of energy. Really get a sense of your heart opening as this ball of energy starts to expand so that it fills your whole chest area

○ Now imagine as you let this ball of energy get even bigger that it starts to fill your whole body

○ Then allow it to get even bigger, so that it expands outward beyond your body and starts to merge with the energy that is all around you

○ Your feet stay anchored on the ground and the ball of energy that you are keeps getting bigger – filling the room that you are in, then the building, then beyond that to the biggest, vastest it can be, way out there, even bigger than the earth, past the planets and connecting to the infinite universe

○ Expand out until you connect to the vibrant light energy, the energy of pure being, connecting to this source energy that holds everything together. Allow yourself to experience this larger dimension

○ When you go out to that space, you can keep connecting and connecting. You don't have an edge or an end to you, you can keep going and going. This is because you are an infinite being in a body who can perceive and know anything and in this space is where you can reprogram anything

- You're centred, anchored by your presence right here in this moment, but you are also connected to that massive outer world of vibrant interconnected energy
- Simply notice and observe how it feels to be in your expanded energy field

6. Raising your vibe to the transformational love vibe

From that expanded place, we can tune into everything, we can reprogram ourselves by shifting to a higher vibe. We are now going to raise our vibration to the love frequency. This is the frequency where transformation and miracles happen.

It takes practice to shift your vibrational frequency, so accept that you are just starting on this journey.

There are many different ways to raise your vibe, and we are going to explore a few. Just go with it and see what works for you.

- Let's start by being grateful for all the love in our lives — say to yourself, "I'm so grateful and thankful for all the love in my life"
- Now tune into one of the ways you experience love in your life. Feel it in your heart and allow your heart to open
- Allow the energy of love to surround you now, feel it, see it and sense it, its colour is usually blue
- Imagine you are downloading it into your whole being. Feel it in your heart and let it spread throughout your body. Allow all of the 70 trillion cells in your body to be bathed in it, step into this energy and say YES to it
- Now say out loud, "I am love." Say it a few times and allow yourself to be the love vibe
- If you were to sound this love vibe, what would the sound be? Just open your throat and let the love vibe sound out
- Now allow this love energy to move your body and dance you, dance your love dance. Do this with your eyes closed for yourself

7. Birthing the new you

Now we are going to use the transformational frequency of love to birth the new version of you that wants to be brought to life.

○ Tune into the magnificent being you really are. Really tune into the energy of who you truly are and the potential it wants to bring into reality. Get a sense of this energy

○ Notice how it feels. What vibe does it have? Sense what qualities are there. Notice how it makes you feel. You may feel unconditional love, pure joy and a sense of being in your true power. Really get in touch with what the potential is for you on your transformational journey

○ Imagine the energy of the new you with all of its potential is right there in front of you and that you can choose to step into it and try it on for size. Take your time to step into it and really embody this energy. Allow it to infuse every cell of your body. Notice how it feels. Open your throat and let out the sound of this new you

○ See yourself bringing this new version of yourself into the world around you. Tune into your knowing to see what the next steps might be, what are you doing, what is happening

○ Now open your eyes, staying connected to the energy of the new you and take it for a walk around the room

○ Notice how it feels to be this new version of yourself, notice how you affect the space, the room and the world around you

○ Set an intention to live as this new you in your daily life

BRINGING THE NEW YOU
INTO YOUR DAILY LIFE

Once you have done the transformational work of bringing the new you into reality, you need to start to bring the new you into your daily life. Exercise 17 uses the Instant Connection Practice to support you in this.

Exercise 17
Bringing the new you
into your daily life

This exercise focuses on the practices that will help you to bring the new you more into your daily life. Set your intention to experience the joy of living life as the new you. Imagine that possibility for yourself and say YES to it.

1. Morning practice

As you are waking up, your brainwaves go from delta, which is deep sleep, to theta, to alpha, to beta and wakefulness. During this waking-up process, the door to your subconscious mind opens up. This is when your brain is most plastic and suggestible.

- Every day as you are waking up and in this theta state, use Instant Connection to get into an expanded state (see below)
- Once expanded, ask what would it be like to be the new you today? How can you live as the new you today?
- Imagine it happening and visualize it
- Don't get up until you feel like that person. Cultivate the emotions of what it feels like to come home to who you really are by opening your heart and feeling the vibration of love, gratitude and joy

By doing this on a daily basis, you will shift your vibration to this state of being. This state will begin to feel familiar to you, and it will become easier for you to access during the day.

2. Daytime practice

When you notice yourself reacting to something and losing connection with the new true you and its high-vibe emotional state, or when you start to close down, use Instant Connection to stay centred and open.

INSTANT CONNECTION

HEAD: Notice your thoughts and make a choice to shift your attention

BODY: Take your awareness down into your body, notice any sensations and allow your body to relax being centred and grounded

WHOLE: Breathe energy into your body, then as you breathe out expand your energy and awareness outward, connecting to the vast energy field around you

○ Once expanded, notice how you're feeling and what is happening in the moment. At first you will just notice and probably not be able to do anything about it. With practice, you will notice a gap opening up and gradually you will be able to make a conscious choice to shift to the vibration of the true you

○ Your job is then to maintain that vibration for as much of your day as possible

In order to keep your channel clear and stop you from closing down, you can use Instant Connection to let go in the moment. Someone says something and you start to feel an early warning sign inside, possibly a tightening (we all have our own particular early warning signs). That's your cue — it's time to grow, not time to protect yourself. Expand using Instant Connection; allow yourself to notice the emotion, don't try to change it, don't fight it and don't judge it. Let it go and release it. You will eventually get conscious enough so that the minute you notice your early warning signal, you stop getting involved with it, you stay centred and open, notice it and let it go.

3. Night-time practice

At night, as you are dropping off to sleep, express your gratitude for the moments of joy and peace that you experienced as you lived the true you during the day.

In short
KEY CONCEPTS TO
TRANSFORM YOUR LIFE

- Transformation is about making a fundamental change, a shift from one state to another, like a caterpillar to a butterfly
- Life is meant to be a series of transformations. The Universe lets us know when we are ready for a transformation
- Emotions are the fuel of transformation and have a role to play at each stage of the transformation journey. Use Exercise 15 (page 216) to accept emotions and transform them to potential
- Enjoying a full life means allowing yourself to experience the high frequency emotions, such as love and joy. Use Exercise 16 (page 222) to experience these high vibe emotions

Try it out for yourself! What are the first steps you intend to take to integrate this into your daily life? Write them down.

Your Reflections

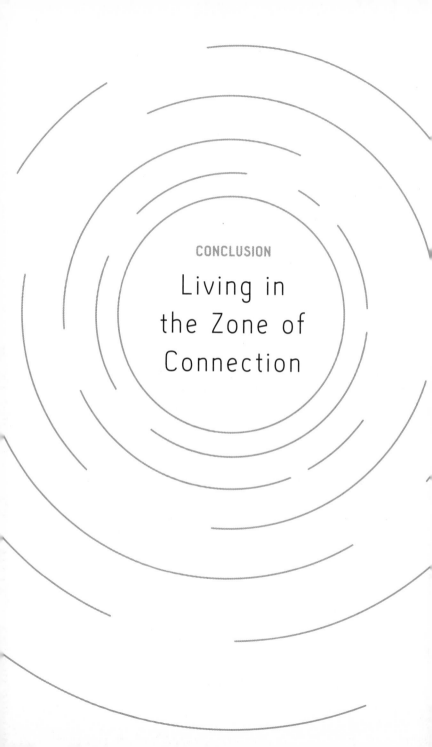

CONCLUSION

Living in the Zone of Connection

THE TRANSFORMATIONAL EFFECT
OF THE CONNECTION PRACTICE

As you practise the exercises throughout this book using the Connection Practice, you will see how it supports you in transforming your life. Through practice and dedication, you will be living in the ZOC. The diagram outlines how it supports you.

The Zone of Connection

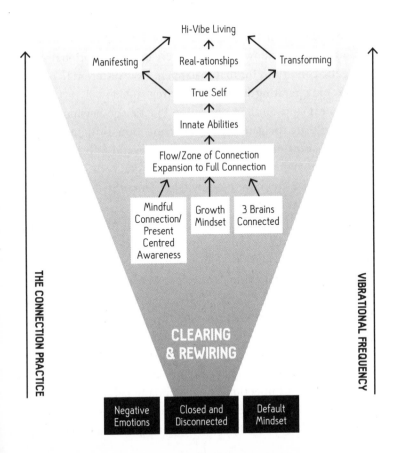

Whenever you experience negative emotions, you are operating from the default mindset and, as a result, are closed and disconnected. The Connection Practice will support you in clearing blocked emotions and rewiring limiting beliefs to create a more empowered growth mindset.

These first steps in using the Connection Practice bring coherence through connecting the three brains and take you to a place of stillness and trust (250 Hz), which we call 'mindful connection'. This allows you to see things from a bigger perspective and accept whatever you are experiencing in the moment. As a result, you are able to use emotions and energy to consciously transform. From this place of acceptance, you can see when something comes up for healing or letting go. Accept that and allow yourself to create the emotional and energetic conditions for that to happen. How different to being in your old operating system and getting stuck!

The next steps in the Connection Practice go beyond mindfulness and are the gateway to full connection, bringing access to higher transformational vibrations (beyond 540 Hz), such as freedom, abundance, joy, peace, bliss, gratitude, enlightenment/oneness. You have now switched from the default to the full connection mindset.

By making the Connection Practice part of your transformational journey, you readily access your sweet spot and a state of flow. From this place of flow, you have access to your innate abilities, such as knowing. Using your knowing, you recognize where you are at each stage of the transformational journey. You are able to sense what the next tiny step forward needs to be rather than being stuck. Your expanded awareness means that you notice the messages and signs from the universe that guide you as to what wants to happen next.

Making the Connection Practice a daily habit brings about internal transformation. This is like reinventing yourself from the inside out, as it starts to rewire your brain and bring the next version of you into being in the world. This 'new you' exists energetically, and it is your job to birth it into reality. That is the ultimate purpose of the transformational journey. As you get in touch with who you really are, your life-force energy flows through you and connects with the wider energy field. You are in your full true power, able to create real-ation-ships, manifest your vision and transform as you evolve to higher vibrational frequencies and awareness. You are in the ZOC, experiencing high-vibe living.

Eventually you are making your own evolutionary shifts on an ongoing basis. In a world that is constantly changing, you are your own disruptor. You are living your full power every day! Each of us has our own journey to make in terms of living from a place of expanded awareness. We know the Connection Practice will be an important tool for you in this process. You may also find that you add in other tools that cross your path and work for you, so be open to whatever will enable you on your journey.

The joy, love, peace and happiness you experience from your inner energy as you transform naturally radiates outward and affects those around you and makes them want to spend time in your presence. You light up your own life and the life of all those you touch. Through this you have a ripple effect because your state affects their state and then their state affects those they come into contact with.

Your ripple effect

—

We know the world is in need of more happiness, peace and love. If you make the inner transformation described in this chapter so that you can experience more peace, love, and joy, you hold the power to transform the collective consciousness and create a more connected, peaceful world. Then you can connect with others at the forefront of the evolutionary shift toward expanded awareness that is the next stage of human development.

You change the world from the inside out! By making the Connection Practice part of your daily routine, you transform yourself and your life and have a transformational effect on those you touch. Living in this way is your journey for the rest of your life. Live each day connected to your full power and unlimited potential. We are very honoured to be on this journey with you and would love to support you in any we can.

Gratitude

Gratitude is a transformative high vibe emotion and one that we love to share as often as possible. We would like to send out our gratitude vibe to all the people who have supported us in bringing this book to fruition.

In writing this book, we drew on a wealth of information from a multitude of sources and the wisdom from many teachers, for which we are most thankful. Worthy of specific mention are:

- Soleira Green, who introduced us to the quantum world and inspired us with her transformational energy-based coaching
- Richard Barrett, for his groundbreaking work in *A New Psychology of Human Wellbeing*
- Wendy Palmer, Loch Kelly, Leora Lightwoman and Eckhart Tolle, for influencing key aspects of our Connection Practice

We are also immensely grateful to all those who experienced the Connection Practice in our workshops, Master Classes and coaching sessions.

We would like to thank Nancy Marriott for writing our book proposal. We were also supported along the way by two experts in the book publishing world – Sophie Bennett and Stephanie Hale. Many thanks to you both.

We have had a wonderful experience working with LID publishing and would like to thank our editor, Sara Taheri, for improving our manuscript and Martin Liu, General Manager of LID, for taking our work out into the world.

Immense gratitude goes to our families. We would not have been able to create this book without the love and support of our children – Alex and Millie Coyne and Emily and Olivia Hutton. Also special thanks go to Jimbo Goodwin for his patience, insight and gentle guiding encouragement throughout the book's conception and birth, and Peter Wroe for support with editing the book and marketing suggestions.

More than anything, though, we offer gratitude to each other. Writing a book on your own is a challenge, but co-writing one, even if it is with your soulmate, is a courageous feat! We are so grateful that collaborating on this book has taken each of us as individuals, as well as our relationship, to a new edge that has meant that we have both grown and unleashed the next level of potential in our real-ationship.

Finally, we offer our gratitude to you, the reader, for buying this book and integrating the Connection Practice into your daily life to make a difference to our beautiful universe.

References

Barrett, Richard, *A New Psychology of Human Well-Being,*
London: Richard Barrett Fulfilling Books, 2016.

Chapman, Gary, *The 5 Love Languages: The Secret to Love that Lasts,*
Chicago: Northfield Publishing, 1995.

Downey, Myles, *Enabling Genius,*
London: LID Publishing, 2016.

Dweck, Carol S., *Mindset,*
New York: Random House, 2006.

Hawkins, David R., *Power vs Force,*
Sedona: Veritas Publishing, 2012.

Land, George, *Breakpoint and Beyond: Mastering the Future – Today,*
New York: HarperBusiness, 1992.

Mental Health Foundation, *Fundamental Facts About Mental
Health 2016,* London: Mental Health Foundation, 2016.

Owen, Nikki, *Charismatic to the Core,*
London: SRA Books, 2015.

Rock, David, *Your Brain at Work,*
New York: HarperCollins, 2009.

Schwartz, Tony and Loehr Jim, *The Power of Full Engagement:
Managing Energy Not Time,* New York: Simon and Schuster, 2005.

Soosalu, Grant and Oka, Marvin, *mBraining: Using Your Multiple
Brains to Do Cool Stuff,* n.p.: mBit International Pty Ltd, 2012.

About the authors

PENNY MALLINSON, MBA

Penny has been at the forefront of personal growth and experiential energy work for over 20 years as a skillful facilitator and visionary coach working with individuals and groups. A love of learning took her from the academic world of an MBA to study self-development in countless forms. Her successful business career and living and working all over the world gives her a broad, refreshing approach.

A true adventurer of the mind, body and spirit, she is passionate about supporting people to shine in their lives. A mother of two incredible girls, she lives between Notting Hill and Dorset, UK, with her beloved husband and dog.

SUE COYNE, PCC

Sue is a successful transformational leadership and team coach, and the author of the bestselling *Stop Doing, Start Leading*. She has also contributed to *Enabling Genius* by Myles Downey, *Leadership Team Coaching in Practice* by Peter Hawkins, and *Leading Beyond the Ego, How to Become a Transpersonal Leader* by John Knights et al.

Meditation and energy work continue to be important elements of Sue's own transformational journey, and she is passionate about sharing the Connection Practice with others to support them on their journey to discover who they really are.